PRESENTED TO

FROM

DATE

Books by

# Wayne Holmes

FROM BETHANY HOUSE PUBLISHERS

---

*The Heart of a Father*
*The Heart of a Mother*
*The Heart of a Teacher*

---

WAYNE HOLMES has served as a children's and youth pastor. His writing has appeared in periodicals and *Ripples of Joy*, a story collection. He directed the Greater Cincinnati Christian Writer's Fellowship for five years and is currently involved with Toastmasters. Wayne, his wife, Linda, and their family live in Cincinnati, Ohio.

# THE
# *Heart*
## of a
# TEACHER

*True Stories of Inspiration
and Encouragement*

*compiled by*
## WAYNE HOLMES

BETHANY HOUSE
Minneapolis, Minnesota

Published by Bethany House Publishers
11400 Hampshire Avenue South
Bloomington, Minnesota 55438

Bethany House Publishers is a division of
Baker Publishing Group, Grand Rapids, Michigan.

Printed in the United States of America

---

**Library of Congress Cataloging-in-Publication Data**

The heart of a teacher : true stories of inspiration and encouragement / compiled by Wayne Holmes.
    p.   cm.
    Summary: "A collection of true stories honoring teachers from the author of The Heart of a Father. These narratives touch the heart while pointing readers to God, the Master Teacher. Each is short enough to read in a sitting, and the stories are ideal devotional readings"—Provided by publisher.
    Includes bibliographical references.
    ISBN 0-7642-2900-1 (hardcover : alk. paper)
    1. Christian teachers—Prayer-books and devotions—English. I. Holmes, Wayne.
BV4596.T43H43    2005
242'.68—dc22                                   2004024209

---

# DEDICATION

*to my wife,*
*Linda Ann Holmes*

# $\mathscr{A}$CKNOWLEDGMENTS

Teachers have influenced my life in innumerable ways. Many of their names—and even some of their faces—have long been forgotten, but their lessons continue to make a difference in my life. From my first recollection of a Sunday school teacher, Bob Graham, to those whose tutelage I am currently under, Cecil (Cec) Murphey, Michael Brewer, Bob Hostetler, and others, I am indebted to them for sharing their gift of teaching.

Some of my teachers have laid down their lesson books. Some have exited the classroom we call humanity to await their final grade. I have no doubt they have passed their exams with ease. I recall with fondness such teachers as "Ducky" McNear and Gary Michelson—teachers and friends who also taught from the example of their lives.

Other names come to mind: Mr. Fellows, Mr. Copeland, Ann Watson, and Dr. Knight. I remember fondly a professor who was no stranger to tears. His lessons were memorable because he felt deeply what he believed and wanted to share those feelings and beliefs. Other teachers—especially the ones I remember—had this special gift of teaching from the heart.

I wish I could recall more of their names and personally say thanks to each one, but I can't. So, to all of those teachers who have given so lovingly and selflessly—

Thank you.

In addition, I want to say thanks to my wife, Linda,
for her loving support.

Special appreciation goes to my agent, Karen Solem.

To Julie Smith, Carol Johnson, and the team at Bethany House,
I extend my gratefulness for their support of this project.

Finally, to all the writers and friends who have supported this book—
some by contributing stories, others by their prayers—
I am indebted to you. May your words and prayers succeed
in touching countless lives to draw them closer
to the heart of the Master Teacher.

*God bless,*

*Wayne Holmes*

# CONTENTS

# $\mathcal{I}$NTRODUCTION

W hen Bonxha (Agnes) Bojaxhiu entered her classroom for the first time in 1931, she did so with no idea how much her teaching—and her life—would affect the world. She had been influenced by a French Carmelite nun who believed it was possible to serve God by doing the most mundane jobs gracefully and cheerfully.

Agnes is more known for the work she did with the poor and dying of Calcutta and is better known by her adopted name chosen because of the French Carmelite nun who influenced her. Mother Teresa, the woman who won the 1979 Nobel Prize for Peace, began her life of ministry as a schoolteacher. The teacher heart of Mother Teresa moved from the small St. Mary's classroom in Calcutta, India, to teach the world about the great heart of God.

Mother Teresa was a teacher. Like all true teachers, she had the special opportunity of making the world a better place. Teachers can impact lives—and sometimes only a single life—but that impact can make a difference in the lives of millions.

*The Heart of a Teacher* celebrates teachers and shares stories from their lives. Many of these stories are from the lives of schoolteachers and professors. Others are from Sunday school teachers, coaches, and mentors. The thread that connects all of these stories is in the way that each teacher reflects the image of God in practical ways.

As you read these narratives I pray you will gain a fresh appreciation for those who have magnanimously dedicated their lives to this distinguished and time-honored calling.

# THE
# *Nurture*
# *of a*
# TEACHER

# THE ALCHEMY OF DREAM DAY

MARK RUTLAND

—— from *Dream* ——

I F GOD IS A DREAMER, which He is, and if He loves dreamers, which He does, then how precious to Him must be those who nurture dreams and dreamers. No mission more productive can be imagined than the raising up of dreamers. One who dreams his own dream does a mighty thing. Those who empower and unleash an army of dreamers are the divine multiplicant of kingdom arithmetic.

I am sprung from a nomadic tribe. My people were movers, frequent movers. In my fifth-grade year we moved to a tough little paper mill town where I felt frightened and out of place. Yet there in a small school that fairly reeked of the nearby mill and in whose halls rough and intimidating sixth-graders made my life miserable, there in that most inglorious setting I met a dream maker, an encourager of hope who impacted my life dramatically. Our teacher, Mrs. Burkett, a sweet but otherwise unremarkable middle-aged school marm, had discovered an alchemy all her own by which she might turn the leaden lumps before her into golden dreamers.

Every first Monday in her class was Dream Day. We loved it. We absolutely adored it and her. On Dream Day we all pulled our little desks into a circle, and one by one we would share our dreams aloud. There were only two rules: Each child had to share a dream, and no one was allowed to laugh at anyone else's.

Some kids changed dreams every month. Mrs. Burkett declared that perfectly acceptable. Some dreams were inane and puny, while others were absurdly unattainable. Somehow, when she spoke, the absurd sounded reasonable, the pedestrian became thrilling, and dreams wildly unreachable by mill-town roughnecks and the semiliterate children of fishermen seemed easily within reach of the least of us.

"I want to be a movie star," breathed Mazie, a hopelessly overweight girl in a faded print dress and dirty sneakers. Anyone who even rolled his or her eyes had to stand in the hall.

"Oh," Mrs. Burkett cooed, "I can't wait. I will sit in a darkened theater with my popcorn. Let's imagine it, class. The lion roars, the credits start and THERE, look, there it is! Starring Mazie Birchfield. Oh, Mazie, I will be so proud."

I stared at the chubby little thing with stringy hair as she fairly squirmed under the tender caress of Mrs. Burkett's affirming voice. Could Mazie? Could she? Ever? Yes, yes, I actually thought it possible. A movie star. Mazie Birchfield suddenly looked different to me. Maybe, just maybe . . .

"Now, who wants to tell their dream next?"

Hands shot up. Now that we had admitted Mazie to the pantheon of international stars, our own young dreams eagerly longed for Mrs. Burkett to take them up onto her ample lap and thus anoint them.

"Me, me!" shouted Danny. "My dream is to be a garbage collector."

*Perfect,* I thought.

"Danny, that is wonderful," she gushed. "I know you will be diligent and careful. You will come on the right day, and you will never, ever leave my can in the street. When my neighbors comment on the wonderful new trash man, I will be so proud to say that I taught him in fifth grade."

Caught up in the dream, we all applauded. Hooray! Hooray for Danny and for garbage men everywhere—a noble race, a great profession. I remember thinking that perhaps I myself might someday want to consider it.

Next was Hugh Don Erlanger, a massive oaf who should have been in eighth grade. "I want to be an astronaut. I want to go up in a rocket ship."

*Yeah, right. Along with the white mice and the chimpanzees.*

"You will!" Mrs. Burkett shouted.

What was she talking about? His I.Q. was exceeded by his shoe size. Was she insane? Hugh Don Erlanger couldn't pass fifth-grade arithmetic or find Florida on the map.

"You will. I just know you will. I will watch you on my TV. Can't you just see it, class? The announcer describes the scene. 'Colonel Erlanger is climbing into the rocket, and the countdown is about to begin.' I am so proud. Suddenly, Colonel Erlanger speaks into his microphone: 'I'd like to thank Mrs. Burkett and all my classmates in Fifth Grade A.' "

Hooray! Hooray, again and again. Colonel Hugh Don Erlanger. An astronaut. Hugh Don sat up straighter, his hulking shoulders squared, and his pathetically dulleyed face fairly glowed. For that moment, if perhaps only for that moment, I, all of us, saw Hugh Don Erlanger differently. His dream, no matter how farfetched, in the magic hands of a dowdy, widowed schoolteacher came alive and danced before us, beckoning our dreams to join the fiesta.

"What about you, Mark?" Her eyes were kindly and inviting. I had never before told anyone my secret, my own private dream kept carefully hidden from mocking eyes. Now I wanted to tell her, as I had hardly ever wanted anything.

"I want to write books." I glared around the room daring anyone, even the hulking astronaut, to so much as snicker.

"And so you shall," she said. "I will look in a bookstore window someday and there it will be; By Mark Rutland it will say, and I will go in and buy it and tell the shopkeeper, 'I taught him, you know. I taught Mark Rutland to write,' and I will be so proud."

I knew it, saw it in her eyes, heard it in her voice and felt it within myself in some secret place deep inside, some place never before touched or awakened. My dream, not just a dream, but my dream, was alive and real for I had seen it in her eyes, looked straight at it and received it. I would never be entirely without it ever again.

# THE SIMPLE FRUITS OF THE SPIRIT

BOB BENSON

from *See You at the House*

*My Father is the gardener . . . I am the vine;*
*you are the branches. . . . Go and bear fruit.*
(JOHN 15: 1, 5, 16)

I ONCE SAW A SIGN on the front of a church that announced, "Our Soul Goal for September is 200." The phrase "soul goal" makes me think of something like scalps or notches on a gun. It does not adequately describe what I believe Jesus was trying to accomplish through us.

Jesus was always aware that souls are packaged in bodies, and they are people. People get cold and hungry and thirsty and lonely. Sometimes they get sick and sometimes they are thrown into prison. And he tells us that they are very important to him, so important that whatever is done or left undone in their behalf was just the same as doing or not doing for him. His life is interwoven with people.

So closely does he identify himself with people everywhere that he tells his disciples, "When they are hungry, I am hungry; when they are cold, I am cold; and wherever you find them, remember that when they bleed, I bleed; when they cry, I cry; when they are thrown into prison, I am thrown into prison. And whatever you do for them, you are doing for me. And whenever you pass them by, you are passing me by."

In the strictest sense, I believe that when we think of bearing fruit we all think first of the Great Commission. We are to go, to bear witness, to baptize, and to teach. Ultimately, the things we do are done to make disciples. We understand that the task is to win souls. Still, it appears to me that even though this was the ultimate or strictest good for Jesus, he went about it in the broadest way possible.

And so I am coming to think that such a strict definition of bearing fruit just doesn't match up very well with all these things he is describing, the "whatever you do for them," that he says are part of the work of the kingdom. They are parts of the processes of God that lead to his redemptive purposes. Anything, even down to a cup of cold water poured in his name, is properly the work of the branches, and branches bear fruit.

I want to make some simple suggestions about "cups of cold water." The first of them is hugs.

For a number of years Peg and I were teachers in the Sunday school. I taught the college class and she taught in the nursery. At present, we are going to class together. I think my fruitbearing still has to find its expression in some way around the church. So my unofficial post is across the hallway just outside the classroom door. We go to early service and then to Sunday school class. After class the hall is filled with people. Those of us who come to the first service are happy because we are ready to go to lunch now. The rest of the people, who are going from class to the sanctuary for the eleven-o'clock service, are also happy because it is always good to be in our worship service.

Now let me tell you that I am, or at least have always wanted to be, a lover. I have never had any disposition at all to be a fighter. A couple of years ago, we were at the class Christmas party at the home of one of the three teachers. I was standing with Wilson, one of my friends, near the front door. The host and hostess were busy elsewhere in the house and, if they didn't hear the doorbell, Wilson and I let the guests in and showed them where to put their coats and how to get to the punch bowl. After a while, he said to me, "Why is it that everybody who comes in shakes my hand and hugs your neck?"

"Well, the reason is simple. When people come in, you hold out your hand. They might want to hug you, but they can't get to you with that big old hand sticking out there. If you would just open your arms, they would walk right into them." And sure enough, after about four more arrivals, he saw my point.

So I was standing at my post in the hall one Sunday after class, ready to serve, when a little old lady whom I have known for a long time came from her class toward me.

She lives alone now because her husband is dead and like the rest of us her children are too busy with their own children to come home much at all. So I opened my arms and she walked right into them. I closed them about her and told her that I loved her. I asked her how she was and she told me. And she went on to church.

Someone told me later that she had heard I had been hugging ladies at church again. When I asked her how she knew, she said, "Birchie came into the sanctuary yesterday morning and sat down beside me. With tears in her eyes, she told me that you had put your arms around her and told her you loved her."

Sometimes it is easy to recruit people for this particular ministry. I was talking about it one evening on a college campus. The next morning was High School Senior Day when kids from all over come to take a look at the school. As I came to chapel that morning, it warmed my heart to see a couple of upperclassmen already putting this good truth into practice. A college could have worse advertising.

At other times, it is a bit more difficult. Every once in a while I go to a church where the pastor says to me, "I sure hope you are not one of those dudes that has us all holding hands." I hate to tell him. Sometimes, when I ask people to join hands, I tell them that Peg and I squeeze each other's hands and that means "I love you." And I ask them to squeeze hands. Not everybody get "squuz." It takes all the courage some people have just to join hands, much less squeeze. I always tell everybody that didn't get "squuz" to see me after church.

And if that is true about joining hands, you can imagine the consternation of a general call to embracing.

I'm afraid you will think I am just a sentimental, weepy-eyed, soft-hearted fool. Well, I am, but what I am saying to you is very, very true.

# I NEVER KNEW HER FIRST NAME

CECIL MURPHEY

I NEVER KNEW MRS. LEAMER'S first name. She became our substitute teacher my first day in third grade. She had light freckles, sandy-colored hair, and wore thick glasses. When she spoke to me, even at age nine, I felt she directed her attention totally to me.

I can't remember anything Mrs. Leamer taught me; but I can never forget the lessons I learned. I was a shy, skinny boy whose clothes never fit properly. What few "new" clothes I had, Mom bought at a second-hand store or they were hand-me-downs from neighbors. Mrs. Leamer didn't pay attention to my clothes; she did pay a lot of attention to me.

One Friday she asked me to stay after school. As soon as the other students had gone, she handed me a book. "I took this from the big library for you." Both of us knew that no students checked out books from the big library until fourth grade.

"It's written on a fifth-grade level," she said, "but I think you can read it. At least, I'd like you to try."

I stared at the book and read the title: *Father's Big Improvements.*

I thanked her (at least I hope I did) and raced from the room. I didn't even wait until I got home to start the book. As I walked the eleven blocks to our house, I read the first two chapters. I had trouble with a few words, but she was right: I could read the book. Monday morning I handed it back to her. "It was good. It was about the father who lived on an old farm and put in electricity and learned to operate a gasoline-powered plow."

She patted my arm. "I knew you could read it."

The following Friday after the final bell rang and all my classmates rushed into the hallway, Mrs. Leamer handed me a book. This time she only smiled and walked away. It was Booth Tarkington's *Penrod*.

I don't know how many weeks this went on, but just before Christmas vacation, she handed me another book, a children's version of *Grimm's Fairy Tales*. "You might want to read this during your vacation."

I smiled gratefully and clasped the book in my hands.

When school resumed in January, we had a different teacher. I laid the book on her desk when she wasn't looking. I never saw Mrs. Leamer again. I'm sure I missed her, but life moved on quickly for us in third grade.

Long after I became a Christian, I thought of Mrs. Leamer. I couldn't remember anything we studied, but I vividly recalled what she did for me. The books, although significant, weren't the most important. She made school a safe place for me, or as I sometimes think of it today, a haven.

Without ever saying such words, Mrs. Leamer made me feel accepted and valued. She didn't see only that shy, skinny kid, but instead focused on my potential—not just who I was, but who I could be. Home was a house of beatings and drunkenness, a place of yellings and unhappiness. My father drank often and sometimes became violent. That fall a serious illness kept him out of work for months. Yet when I walked into Mrs. Leamer's classroom, I could push that part of my life behind me. For those hours, I escaped from loneliness, poverty, and isolation. I was safe and someone cared about me. Beginning with those days in third grade and continuing all the way through high school, once I walked inside the school building I tuned out my miserable home life.

Years later, I tried to locate that special teacher; unfortunately, the school system no longer kept records dating back that far. Even though she entered and left my life within a three-month period, she had given me hope.

In a way, that's how Jesus Christ operates, isn't it? Jesus has always known my potential. Through the years, he sent people into my life—individuals like Mrs. Leamer—to nurture and encourage me. Those special individuals enabled me to inch toward feeling accepted and worthwhile.

I never knew her first name, but I know God does. I felt as if God had prepared me for wholeness and acceptance. One of those who helped was a woman whose first name I never learned.

# BUDDY FILMS

RUSTY FISCHER

IT WAS ANOTHER FRIDAY, five-o'clock twilight show, and was I ever ready. After a week of teaching computer skills to kindergarten to sixth-graders, I needed nothing more than two pure hours of car chases, machine guns, a family tub of popcorn, and a garbage-can-size soda to ease me far from reality.

As the previews rolled in the nearly empty theater, I heard flip-flops flip-flapping down the aisle behind me and recognized them as belonging to a student: If they didn't belong to one of my students, they surely belonged to *somebody's* student.

In fact, as the flip-flapper passed by the middle seats in favor of the front row, I recognized the back of Bernie's head. He had a cowlick that extended above his forehead like a geyser—and always leaned to the left.

"Great," I thought, already covered in popcorn kernels, "now I've got to leave early before Bernie spots his dorky computer teacher seeing a movie—alone—on a Friday night."

Too late. Bernie must have forgotten something at the concession stand and was already flip-flapping back up the aisle.

"Okay," I thought, "the lights are too low for him to—"

"Mr. Fischer?" barked Bernie. "What are *you* doing here?"

With that, Bernie remembered he had to go buy a candy bar before the movie started.

By the time he got back, the movie was rolling and Bernie ignored me on his way down the aisle. (Students have a way of doing that.) Fortunately, I escaped during the credits without having to explain to a sixth grader why his teacher was such a loser.

Next Friday, as was my habit, I was seated midway down a mostly empty theater for yet another twilight show. Another shoot 'em up, another fading film star flexing sagging muscles, and plenty of special effects to suck the stress out of my tired-teacher brain.

By the time the previews were starting, there was Bernie's cowlick bouncing up and down in the flickering lights. This time, he didn't look back as he flapped his way down the aisle. "Hey, Mr. F.," he shot over his shoulder casually.

Embarrassed to be caught alone once more, I was glad the house lights were already down. After that, Bernie and I got in a routine. Somehow, every week, we ended up at the same movie—at the same time. Like me, Bernie had a fondness for action-adventure, sci-fi, and horror.

I never wondered why Bernie was able to skate into grown-up monster or sci-fi flicks as easily as he flipped and flapped his way down the aisle. He was obviously smart enough to fool the dense teenager camped behind the ticket booth, or he simply bought a ticket to the latest Disney flick and skirted past the just-as-dimwitted usher in his fake tux and plastic shoes.

"TGIF, Mr. Fischer," Bernie would wink each week as he flapped down the aisle.

"Sure thing, Bernie," I would mumble in reply.

As fall turned to winter and the holiday blockbusters roared into town, Bernie's cowlick, outlined in the flickering movie screen, inched its way closer until, finally, halfway through January, Bernie allowed himself to sit in my row.

Over the crunching of popcorn and the blaring of gunfire, I realized that Bernie and I had a lot in common. While the rest of the sparse afternoon audience laughed easily at tired punch lines, Bernie and I were more apt to laugh at the unintentional blunders of these low-budget flicks. We were often greeted with turned heads and the occasional "shhh."

Bernie and I only laughed harder, unable to control ourselves.

At school, Bernie and I rarely spoke. He was only in my rotating computer course twice a week, and my favorite sixth grader had little time for his movie buddy during school. But in that darkened theater, I developed a special fondness for little Bernie—his easy laughter, his keen intelligence, his addiction to blood and guts. We both hated Meg Ryan and the *Mission Impossible* series, but were easy suckers for anything with vampires—or J.Lo.

One week after spring break, the doors burst open and Bernie plunged into the seat next to me, not even leaving an empty seat so each of us could have our own armrest.

"We're moving, Mr. F.," he blurted out nervously, the torn ticket still clutched in his hand. "My dad got a promotion. They're moving him to the Dallas plant."

"When are you leaving?" I asked.

"Next Sunday," he murmured. "You know what *that* means?"

I frowned. It meant so many things.

"Only one more TGIF!" he said sadly, reaching into my bag for a handful of popcorn. My teacher's smile must have confused him, but I was upset and didn't know what else to do.

When Bernie didn't show for our last TGIF, I assumed he was just late. But the previews came, the previews went, and still no Bernie. *Long line at the concession stand*, I fretted, straining my neck to look over the empty seats behind me. The movie started, and I sat through another low-budget zombie flick alone. My popcorn went uneaten—a first—and I only drank the soda to drown the heaviness in my chest.

The next Monday at school, I asked the secretary about Bernie. "Oh, he had to transfer early," she murmured. "I'll need his grade."

"A," I said quickly.

"An A? For Bernie? He gets straight D's in all his other classes."

"Really? But he's so smart!"

"Are we talking about the same Bernie?" she asked. "The kid with ADD? The kid who's sitting in the principal's office once a week? The kid who'll probably have to repeat sixth grade?" It was a long week for me, with no Bernie to look forward to on Friday. As my favorite day of the week dawned bright and early, I mumbled through several unenthusiastic "TGIFs" from my fellow teachers as we milled about the crowded teachers' lounge. Rifling through the lunch menus and catalogs in my dusty cubby, I noticed an envelope with a Texas postmark.

Ripping it open, I found five dollars' worth of movie gift certificates and Bernie's handwriting scrawled across a sheet of notebook paper: "Sorry about our last movie, Mr. F. But see one on me. (I hope you know these came out of my allowance.) I never knew how close Texas was to California. Can I use you as a reference on my application to film school? Keep looking for me in the credits. Bernie."

As the years pass, I've made it a habit to stay for the credits. It annoys my beautiful wife to no end, but having heard the story a hundred times by now, she too dutifully scans those rolling names each week.

"Don't you remember his last name?" she occasionally asks as the theater drains and the ushers clean up around us.

Unfortunately, the years have robbed me of that information, and all I can look for is "Bernie."

————

Bernie and I formed a special bond that year. Skating past the ticket takers, whiling away time in a darkened theater, eating too much popcorn, and moving in our own little world, we found a way to relieve the pressures of everyday life and rest in the comfort of each other's company. I often wonder if God doesn't occasionally call us to a similar form of rest—moving together past the ticket takers of life to while away the hours in his presence—sometimes in a darkened room, doing nothing more than taking in the scenes of life as they unfold.

# THAT EXTRA MILE

## ANITA HIGMAN

HIGH SCHOOL CAN GET MESSY. And if the usual teenage angst is compounded with a slight weight problem, heavy eyeglasses, acne, and poor self-esteem, a coming-of-age scene can play out that may not delight all those in attendance. That pretty well describes some of my high school years.

Then entered Mrs. Brymore. Being around her was like being wrapped in flannel pj's, warm and comforting. I could feel her smile coming before she entered a classroom. Her laughter was free and flowing, like a kite released in a breeze. I can't remember how she looked with a frown. I know she surely had one at some point, yet I can't think how it looked. Mrs. Brymore was simply gifted at smiling.

When she taught, I never felt like a laboratory container that merely had to be filled with information. With her caring and camaraderie, I knew that we were more than students. We were precious folk she genuinely liked to be around.

Trust always reigned supreme on Mrs. Brymore's list of attributes. She was not only credible, but she fostered that quality in others. One summer, she rescued me from pretty miserable waitressing work by offering me a job as her helper at the school's library. I was to help revamp the entire library at our school. Mrs. Brymore gave me my instructions, made sure I was comfortable with them, and then never once glared over my shoulder as if waiting for me to fail. Her eyes always said, "I know you can do this, Anita." She placed more confidence in me than I did in myself. What a boost that summer was to the faltering ego of a lip-chewing teenager.

Mrs. Brymore was also one of the finest examples of Christian womanhood I have ever known. She never spread negative barbs or bits of gossip, but instead sprinkled encouragement, biblical wisdom, kindness, and truth all around her.

Her advice ranged from the profound to the practical. Once when she saw I was trying to impress a young man, she mentioned how wise it would be to remove the gum from my mouth. Apparently, in my fervor to claim his affection, I'd created a real open-mouthed smacking commotion that could be experienced from quite a distance. I thanked her for her keen observations and quickly removed my gum.

The profound parts of her life were not only in her godly counsel, but in her Christ-like example in the everyday stuff of life. She was truly a living monument I could admire in my youth and aspire to be like as an adult.

Without this dear teacher in my growing-up years, I may have drifted, grown weary, or just quietly given up my goals. I only know that when I think of Mrs. Brymore, I think of someone God must have been able to use readily for his purposes for bettering my life and the many young people who had been entrusted in her care. What a blessing to encounter this woman who desired to really make a positive difference. On a more personal level, she was someone who believed in me enough to make me feel I was a likeable and valuable human being with God-given potential.

I'm grateful to God for placing Mrs. Brymore along my early path. As I reflect on her life as an extraordinary instructor, I like to think I figured out her most basic secret. The main ingredient was so simple, yet deeply significant: Mrs. Brymore always went that extra mile. She didn't just instruct, she nurtured. She never punished, but instead guided with caring discipline. She didn't just watch over her students, she genuinely loved them. The gathering of knowledge was important, the classroom time necessary, but her willingness to go beyond books with a sincere, serving attitude was even more vital. Mrs. Brymore's influence in my life was not a one-time story or a telling of a crossroads moment with her at the helm, but a mosaic of good and godly pieces placed each day into the life-picture of what she hoped I would become.

In fact, Mrs. Brymore gave me an even more important heart-treasure—a glimpse into God's character. Our loving Creator goes that extra mile too. He doesn't just teach us how to behave and journey on this earth, but loves us enough to nurture us, guide us, and provide us with the gift of eternal life, because he too sees us as precious folk he genuinely likes to be around.

# THE
# EXAMPLE
## of a
# TEACHER

# $\mathscr{P}$ATIENCE

PENELOPE J. STOKES

—∽ from *Simple Words of Wisdom* ∿—

*Patience is a bitter plant but it has a sweet fruit.*
(GERMAN PROVERB)

T HE OLD PROFESSOR SAT IN his office, surrounded by papers that needed grading and piles of mid-term exams. He had been trying for weeks to finish an article for a scholarly journal, and the outline still sat next to his typewriter, untouched.

A knock sounded on the door, and he shook his head impatiently. Why couldn't he get a few moments of peace? Just a little time to finish that article and catch up on his paperwork . . .

He sighed and said, "Come in."

The door opened to reveal a young woman—a student in one of his classes. She was a bright girl, with a promising future, but she needed some direction. "Am I interrupting your work?" she asked timidly, staring around at the mass of unfinished work that cluttered the office. "I could come back some other time."

The professor looked into her face and saw that familiar expression of hope and anticipation. And suddenly he remembered why he had gone into teaching in the first place. "Yes, you're interrupting," he said. "But come in. Interruptions *are* my work."

We are an impatient people, even those of us who claim the name of Christ. We have a hard time seeing beyond our schedules, our responsibilities, our well-ordered plans and goals.

Patience is the kind of character trait that everyone wants to possess but no one wants to develop. And it's no wonder. The Bible tells us that suffering brings patience, (Rom. 5:3) so we don't dare pray for patience lest suffering come. The truth is, we want what we want when we want it. We don't like sitting in traffic. We're frustrated and demoralized by delayed gratification and unanswered prayer. We want patience, but we want it *right now*.

But patience is, by its very nature, a future-oriented virtue. "If we hope for what we do not yet have," Romans 8:25 tells us, "we wait for it patiently." Hebrews encourages us to "imitate those who through faith and patience inherit what has been promised" (Heb. 6:12).

Patience, it seems, is developed in the Christian life through two processes—*delay and interruption*. Neither is very attractive to goal-driven, product-oriented twentieth-century people like us. But our responses to both are based on faith. Faith in God's timing, and faith in God's priority system.

If we want to be people of patience, we need to trust that God is in control of the outcome. What we call a detour may be the Lord's scenic turnpike. When our plans are delayed by gridlock or interrupted by unanticipated re-routing, God knows the best way home.

# BRIEF ENCOUNTER

SUZANNE SCHRYVER

T HE ARID HEAT OF THE California desert stings my nose as I
attempt a run along the Sacramento River trail in Redding. The dry
heat burns my lungs, but I push myself on, listening to the rhythmic beat
of my footsteps on the steaming asphalt.

Before I moved to this somewhat rural part of California, I was warned
about the heat, but I shrugged off the warnings. How bad could it be? I'd
wondered from my naïve position of youthful adventure seeker. After all,
the dog days of summer in New England could be sweltering with their
smothering humidity. What I hadn't anticipated was four straight months
of highs well above 100 degrees and an apartment with an air-conditioning
unit that was sluggish on even the coolest of days. The 85-degree heat
inside was a welcome break from the outdoor oppression when I first
entered, but I grew uncomfortable and irritated after only a few short
minutes.

Regardless of the heat, my body and mind crave the exertion of a run
and the freedom that comes from being outdoors. Some days when school
ends, I run this route with a fellow teacher or a group of other runners.

But today I am on my own, passing a smattering of other runners, walkers, and in-line skaters on my journey.

Running has become a welcome time of day—a time when I am alone with myself and my thoughts. I can clear my mind of the clutter of the day and prepare myself for the job of grading papers and planning lessons for the days to come. Or I can think of nothing and merely enjoy the river flowing beside me and the changes in my path. It is my time to reconnect with myself after a long, demanding day of dealing with my teenage students and the issues they face.

Dusk is approaching. A murky grayness settles over the earth while the sky above fades from bright to pale blue. I reach the footbridge that is my landmark. Despite the heat, I have just completed an effortless two miles, and I will turn here and complete my run back to the small parking lot.

As I run back, I notice for the first time the bright gold coin of the moon floating against the sky, watching me, following me, giving me energy to complete my run. A sense of wonder and magic overtake my body in a thrill of goose bumps at the beauty of God's world. The air is cooling to near comfortable when I detect a rustling in the brush up ahead. I slow my pace and stop, my breath hard and heavy from the sudden halt of my exertion. I strain my eyes and see the motion of a gray figure on the bank above me.

A shadowy face peers at me through the dried weeds, determines I pose little threat, and begins its descent over the uncertain gravel. Out of the translucent dusk, the fuzzy image emerges as the form of a deer, then two, and finally, three. I relax into an all-encompassing sense of God's peace and serenity as these graceful animals allow me to share their space in the dusk of a long day.

As I watch, motionless, the trio slip fluidly down the gravel bank, stirring up more noise than I expect in a magical moment such as this. Twelve bony hooves cross the paved path. I stand still and stare in awe at these creatures as each pauses on the path, glances my way, and returns to picking its way through the grassy meadow standing between it and a refreshing drink of the cool water of the river.

I strain to maintain sight of the trio as the final figure disappears into the stillness of the evening. For several more seconds, I stand transfixed, enfolded in God's soothing presence. Finally, I run on, finishing my workout in the haze of wonder that this momentary connection with such beautiful creatures of nature has reminded me of God's desire to transform even the most mundane aspects of my life.

In the morning, the encounter is still fresh in my mind as I enter the rough-hewn building that houses my classroom, nestled in the foothills of the Cascade Mountains. My students wait in sleepy anticipation, knowing that we always begin class with the same brain-clearing activity. "Take out your notebooks," I announce. "We'll do a ten-minute freewrite." Several students appear relieved. Those few still reluctant to write without a clear assignment register their annoyance with sighs and moans, but they begin writing anyway.

I too join the writing, believing that we lead by example. On this morning, my pen flows easily and quickly over the page as I transport myself back to my run of the evening before, recounting my experience and my feelings at sharing a simple but intimate moment with three of nature's more beautiful and graceful creatures. I glance at the clock occasionally so I won't exceed the ten-minute time.

When writing time is up, students have the opportunity to share their writing, and, as usual, I read too. I feel strongly that my comfort in reading my own hastily scrawled first-draft writing will help make them more comfortable reading their own work. My students listen intently, experiencing the sights and feelings that I have re-created. For a moment, God's peace flows from my experience and settles over my students.

I finish reading and the room is silent for a second longer than my comfort level allows. I shuffle my papers and begin to stand, preparing to move into the lesson when John pipes up, "That didn't really happen, did it?"

"Yes," I nod. "Last night when I went home."

"That's really cool," someone else says.

"Yeah," I say. "It surprised me too." I pause for a minute. "Okay. Take out your lit books and turn to page 192."

"Ms. Schryver?" Rachel says, and I turn, eyebrows raised in question.

"Yes, Rachel?"

"Thanks for sharing."

I smile, hearing my own words flowing from her lips. I know she means it—not just sharing my writing, but sharing my experience. My life and my faith. And sharing on that level means that if I'm in the classroom, God is in there with me.

# SILVER THREADS AMONG THE GOLD

LANITA BRADLEY BOYD

L AWRENCE STOPPED THE NURSE who was walking briskly
down the tastefully decorated corridor. "We're here to visit Mrs.
Moore," he said, hesitating over the seldom-used title. "Does she—does
she recognize people?"

The nurse shook her head, showing none of the brusqueness Lawrence
and Mary expected. "Miss Marie?" she asked, and he nodded, surprised to
hear the Southern use of "Miss" with the first name. "Not really. Sometimes we think she does understand even when she doesn't respond. On
rare days she seems to know her daughter. It breaks our hearts. You know,
lots of us here at the nursing home had her as a teacher at one time or
another. She was unique. She was a classy lady, all right." She smiled fondly.
"There was a time that there wasn't a sharper mind than hers anywhere."

Lawrence and Mary looked more closely at the nurse, the familiarity
of her tone drawing their attention. "Do I know you?" Lawrence asked,
hesitantly.

"You should, Mr. Bradley. I was Norma Faye Atchinson, now Parks. I
had you for biology the same year I had Miss Marie for algebra. You
haven't changed all that much, but I know I sure have. I wouldn't have

expected you to recognize me with all this weight. And I have children of my own in high school too. Just last week I was telling my daughter, who's taking sophomore biology, how interesting your classes were."

Her sudden girlish giggle placed him instantly back in the sultry biology lab of many years before, watching a group of girls whispering and giggling over the new yearbook.

"Do you notice we still say 'Miss Maa-rie' like she always did? When new girls come in and start calling her 'Mrs. Moore' or just 'Muh-rie'—can you imagine such disrespect?—we straighten them out right away. We say 'This is Miss Maa-rie, who was a childhood friend of Madame Chiang Kai-shek and the best teacher Sumner County High School ever had. You be sure you show her the proper respect. And pronounce her name right!' And you'd better believe they do!"

They smiled, then moved on into Miss Marie's room.

The aristocratic white head rested lightly on the spotless pillow, its fragility heightening the impression of elegance. They stood at each side of the bed.

"Miss Marie, it's Lawrence," he said. "Mary and I came by to say hello. You have a nice neat place here."

The old eyelids fluttered slightly. She stared blankly at each of them in turn, giving no sign of recognition.

Lawrence spoke at length of days past—rushing from topic to topic, wondering if she was understanding anything. He talked about the Tennessee high school where they had taught, of students and teachers they had known, of more current happenings since they'd both left—she to retire, he to another school. He scanned her face for any sign of recognition.

"Times are so different now, Miss Marie. The students are different, and they're under so much pressure. Going to school isn't like it used to be when we were teaching together. Parents now don't have the same respect for education as the parents we dealt with. That shows in the way the students act too.

"You and I used to sing some pretty good duets at those school talent shows, didn't we? We don't even hear most of those old songs anymore, but everyone loved them back then. Remember 'The Rose of Tralee' and 'Silver Threads Among the Gold'? And how about 'I'll Take You Home Again, Kathleen'? Your voice was fantastic. I still think of you when I hear a clear, melodic voice that can really master those high notes."

He looked pleadingly at his wife, and she nodded, knowing he wanted support in this one-sided conversation. "Our children are all doing well, Miss Marie. They all loved having you in school. You know, that last year you taught, Lanita changed her whole four-year plan of courses so she could take as many classes as possible from you. You're just about a saint to everybody you ever taught, I guess." Mary stopped abruptly, her voice catching, and shrugged as she looked sadly at Lawrence.

Lawrence began again, pondering each phrase, pausing frequently. "I think that for all of us who had grown up in the country and had never been very sophisticated, we were glad just to get to sit at your feet. You knew something about everything. We'd never had a teacher who could teach Latin and English literature and algebra equally well. You had such style, such verve about everything you ever did. You taught us to respect God and each other. You taught us all that *what* we do in life is not more important than *how* we do it."

Lawrence and Mary looked at the delicately waved white hair resting on the immaculate pillow and then at each other.

"I guess we'll be going now," Lawrence said. "I don't really know if you've understood any of this. They were just things I should have said to you long ago and never did. You were such a great influence on my life when you were my teacher, and then even more when we taught together. You really made me understand about teenagers and caring.

"Until we had all those long conversations about students and teaching, I had never had a glimmer of understanding why you were so successful with every student, no matter what their backgrounds or needs. You taught me that demanding only the best from each of them showed caring most of all. You were always my role model, and I felt like I had to come and tell you so. Any success I have had as a teacher I owe to you."

The frail body remained motionless, eyes closed.

"I hope you understood some of this." He paused, watching for some response. "Good-bye now."

Hand in hand, the couple walked slowly toward the door, hesitant to leave, yet seeing the futility of staying. Suddenly they were stopped by a gentle quavering sound from the bed.

"Dah-ling, I am grow-ing o-old. Sil-ver threads among the gold," the aged voice sang. Lawrence moved instantly to her side. The blue eyes fluttered open as his gentle tenor joined her wispy soprano. "Shine upon my brow to-da-ay; life is fading fast a-way.

"But, my dah-ling, you will be-e-e, Al-ways young and fair to me. Yes, my dah-ling, you will be-e, Always young and fair to me."[1]

Her voice gained strength and her enunciation was flawless when they reached the chorus. Lawrence grasped the fragile hand. "Dah-ling, I am growing o-old, Silver threads among the gold. Shine upon my brow today; Life is fading fast away."

Miss Marie smiled softly, her eyes now closed again. The effort had obviously drained her limited strength, but they sensed that for her it had been worth it. Her student, her mentee, her friend, had come to pay tribute, and she had responded, as always, with style.

As they returned to the car, Lawrence thought about how Miss Marie had shown him God through her example and her teaching. He thanked God for allowing him to have this inspiring moment with her, for guiding their time together both in the past and today. Gratefully, he contemplated God's incalculable blessings and instruction through one of his beloved children, the extraordinary Miss Marie.

---

[1]"Silver Threads Among the Gold," Melody by Hart Pease Danks, 1834–1903, lyrics by Eben E. Rexford, 1848–1916.

# MISS RITTER'S BIBLE

LUCIA ST. JOHN

ALMOST ALWAYS SHE WORE a simple black dress, but the black only made her gentle, smiling face shine ever more brightly. A splash of white trimmed her hemline because, almost always, her slip showed. What I remember most about my first-grade teacher is that always at her side was her big black Bible.

The year was 1951, and I was a pupil in Miss Ritter's lively class at Roosevelt Public School in Norristown, Pennsylvania. Every morning, just before the beginning of lessons, Miss Ritter took her big black Bible and opened it to the twenty-third Psalm.

"Boys and girls, please rise."

Immediately we slid out of our seats and stood straight as soldiers. Not a student spoke or squirmed as our teacher slowly read the comforting words. We instinctively knew that we had entered the presence of God.

Miss Ritter's melodious voice rang throughout the room. "The Lord is my shepherd; I shall not want."

The words calmed my spirit. Although I didn't fully comprehend their meaning, I felt their healing balm flow over my troubled soul like warm oil.

Despite my tender years, I had known much want: want of unconditional love, want of peace, and, on occasion, even want of food. Living in a home with serious problems, I had become an anxious, wounded lamb, untrusting and afraid. Instead of knowing the care of the loving Shepherd, I knew rejection and pain.

Day after day, as Miss Ritter faithfully read the twenty-third Psalm, a dream began to birth within me. Would this wonderful Shepherd my teacher read about every day want to become *my* Shepherd? I wondered. How I longed for someone who would take care of me, who would never abandon me, and whom I could trust with all my heart.

For some of my classmates, the Bible didn't merit particular attention, but it became the focus point of my attention. I had never seen a Bible until Miss Ritter introduced the class to hers.

The way my beloved teacher treasured that book drew me to it. She treated her Bible with the highest respect and demonstrated great love for what it held within its pages. Little did I realize then that her example would birth in me an abiding love for the Holy Book and a deep hunger for what it contains.

I recognized in Miss Ritter's daily reading of the twenty-third Psalm the marvelous love of God for a hurting little girl. In giving me this godly teacher, he provided me with a link to his love—a love I desperately needed.

More than fifty years later, the words of that beloved psalm still ring in my ears. I remember little about first grade, but I vividly remember Miss Ritter. More important, I shall never forget her big black Bible. Watered by her prayers, the seed of the Word of God she planted within me during that impressionable year has taken root and, by God's grace, has produced much fruit. The dream she inspired in me has come true. The Shepherd of Psalm 23 is now my Shepherd.

# THE
# DISCIPLINE
# of a
# TEACHER

# BACK OF THE ROOM

NANCY ELLEN HIRD

MARCUS WAS A KID YOU noticed right away. He made you notice him. Gregarious, fun-loving—his future had talk-show host or stand-up comic written all over it. His present, however, was upstaging my lesson plans. My seventh-grade social studies class preferred his jokes and buffoonery to longitude and latitude.

At first I laughed along good-naturedly. But Marcus took that as a cue to step up his performances. That encouraged other students. Before long five of them were vying with him for their moments in the spotlight. I began to rein in the class. I also tried reasoning with Marcus.

I told him that while we enjoyed his humor, we all needed to give more attention to learning how to read maps and recognize the countries and continents. "You're keeping the others from focusing on the lessons. And, Marcus, your own work recently has become less than great. It's half-done, it's sloppy, and sometimes it's even late."

Marcus listened but then made excuses.

In class he continued to be disruptive. I benched him during lunch recesses. It didn't deter him. He was out of control.

How much out of control I didn't grasp until the day the principal visited my classroom. Recklessly Marcus continued his outbursts even in front of him.

The principal pointed at Marcus. "Follow me. I want to talk with you."

Marcus got up, started to follow, then turning, quipped to the class, "Good, 'cause I want talk to him too."

Some of the kids snickered; others looked as horrified as I felt.

"That's it, Marcus. You're suspended," I said.

For a long moment, he stared at me, his eyes big and unbelieving. Then seeming to remember he had an audience, he swaggered out the door with a who-cares attitude. I was stunned.

As the day wore on, however, I began to question myself. Had I over-reacted? Marcus was after all a good kid. Maybe I should have had more patience with him. He was young. This clowning was only a phase. He would outgrow it naturally, wouldn't he?

The sixth-grade teacher caught up with me after school. "I heard you suspended Marcus."

"Yes," I said sheepishly.

"I'm glad. It should have happened before this. He's basically a good kid, but he gets out of control and doesn't know what to do. Maybe we'll help him figure it out this time."

At the parent-teacher conference Marcus was thoughtful. His bravado had vanished. He admitted that he got too wound up, that once the class started laughing at him, he couldn't stop himself. He also admitted that it was interfering with his getting his work done.

We decided that he should change his seat assignment to the back of the room where he could concentrate more on doing his schoolwork and less on entertaining the class.

On his first morning back, just before class started, he came up quietly to my desk.

"About what we talked about the other day at the parent-teacher conference ..."

"Yes."

"Well," he lowered his voice and looked over his shoulder, "I want to do it, but could you please send me there?"

I blinked, not understanding his request. Then I got it. But should I play the scene? I decided if it would help Marcus, I would do it. "Okay," I agreed.

He went back to his desk and almost immediately began a boisterous conversation with a kid across the room.

"Marcus," I said sternly, "take your books and papers and move to the desk in the back. From now on, that will be your seat."

He glared at me, aware that every eye in the room was on him. Then he grabbed his things and sauntered toward the back. Scene over, his classmates went back to work.

Marcus turned his face toward me. "Thank you," he mouthed.

From that day Marcus's schoolwork improved dramatically. He turned in assignments that were carefully done, complete, and on time. He became good friends with another hardworking student. They approached me one morning and asked if they could sit together. I said I would agree if they would promise to get their work done without disturbing everyone around them. They said they would and they did—usually. In fact Marcus' attitude and work improved so much that his other teachers and I decided he could do more advanced work.

Four months later Marcus and I were sitting outside the gym during a basketball tournament.

"You know," he said to me, "what you did suspending me and moving me to the back of the room, it was hard for me. It was really hard for me at first."

I nodded, uneasy about what he would say next.

"But it really helped me. I got to thank you. I really got to thank you."

I smiled. Actually, I glowed all the way home.

I wonder if God ever sends us to the back of the room. Like Marcus, we sometimes get into situations where temptations are just too tempting.

We need to make a change, but we can't muster the strength. God, reading our hearts, lovingly makes it for us.

Proverbs 3:12 makes it plain: "... the Lord disciplines those he loves, as a father the son he delights in."

# THE UGLY TRUTH

KAY DEW SHOSTAK

T WO HUGE RED LETTERS covered every page of my first college research paper. Being a good Southern girl, I'd never said those two letters to anyone, and I'd most definitely never said the words they stood for.

I returned to the classroom shaking my head. I held the paper toward the teacher, Mr. Atkinson—my favorite teacher until five minutes earlier.

Birth defects had marked him with twisted legs, bent arms, and an enlarged head. Thick black-rimmed glasses constantly had to be pushed back into place, but despite all this, his most noticeable attribute was a toothy grin. Shuffling through the halls, he bantered with students and teachers, often laughing about his infirmities. In class he was riveting. He taught psychology and enlivened every lecture with insight from his special view of the human race.

It was my first quarter in college, and he was everything a professor should be.

I'd sailed through high school, working my own special system. Bs were attainable with no work, so Bs filled my report cards. Math I found more difficult, but I arranged to get in the slow classes with low expectations.

My English teachers seemed to prefer quantity to quality, so I provided lots and lots of words.

Once I pointed this out to a friend who strived for As. He complained when his paper on John Donne's "No Man is an Island" received a B, while mine got an A. We both knew his was a better paper, so I revealed his failing. "You didn't make it long enough." He was incredulous, but later papers proved me right.

Now, I held my first college paper and it didn't even have a grade, just two letters, eleven inches tall, in bright-red marker.

Maybe it was a joke by some student helping grade papers. I held the paper out for him to see. "I don't understand, Mr. Atkinson."

He turned his unwieldy head toward me and one eyebrow peeked above the black rim of his glasses. He grinned and nodded. "It is, isn't it?"

"What?" I asked, more confused than ever.

"Your paper. It's just what I wrote, right?"

I opened my mouth to argue, but then looked down at the words behind his red letters. The words upon words upon words, and I knew it—he was right.

"Do the paper again and bring it back to me tomorrow." He turned back to his work and I returned to the hallway.

Late that night I sat at my desk. My other homework completed, only the red-marked paper lay in front of me. I wanted to plead ignorance and throw my hands up in disgust at this impossible-to-please teacher. Perhaps his deformities made him think he could get away with this kind of thing. Maybe putting down lowly first-year students made him feel powerful. He probably got a good laugh at my squirming. I gripped my pen and slammed my hand on the desk, "I just don't know what he wants from me."

Lies, so familiar, rushed to my mind. *This is the best I can do. Other people are just smarter than I am. Besides, nobody really cares as long as there are enough words.*

However, the lies couldn't drown out the truth: This teacher had my number. Multitudes of words, smiles, and enthusiasm—some of my best defenses—he shoved aside just as effortlessly as he pushed his glasses back in place.

My pen tapped quickly on the edge of the desk. *Now what do I do?* Clean white pages waited, but the glaring red slashes held my attention. *What if I do my best and it comes back marked up like this?*

Slowly, however, distaste for Mr. Atkinson's ugly comment worked to edge out my fear of rejection. Usually encouraging words, kind comments, and gold stars spur students to work harder; but those I ate like ice cream, always looking for easier ways to get more. Now a dose of castor oil prodded and poked at me.

His opinion of my work was ugly, but it was true.

Shame and embarrassment punched through my smugness. My self-designed system showed itself to be shoddy and cheap. Garnering as much praise for as little work as possible suddenly didn't look like such a great life plan.

I gathered the red-marked pages, straightened them, folded them twice, and put them in the garbage can.

I placed the clean sheets in front of me and began again. This time, however, my writing required concentration. I pushed thoughts of pleasing the teacher out of my mind and focused on my observations and thoughts. At first my mind wandered and I'd find myself writing on autopilot. Frustrated, I'd pull myself back, determined to fully engage in the writing.

Deep into the paper I lost track of time. When I finished the last page, the clock showed I'd been working for five hours. Yet I felt less tired than when I first sat down. I stretched and grinned—I hadn't expected these feelings. Pride for the pages lying on my desk drowned out the creeping fear of rejection. My brain felt like an underused muscle that finally got a good workout. I was tired, but satisfied.

As I turned off my light and crawled into bed my smile only grew. Since when did working hard make you feel so good?

However, Mr. Atkinson apparently knew the connection because when I handed him my paper the next morning he had a question for me. "Did you have fun?" Before I could respond, he peered over his thick lenses and grinned. "I'll get this back to you tomorrow, but I know it will be fine." Throwing the paper on one of the many piles overflowing his desk, he sat down to begin class.

The next day he returned the paper. He gave it an A, and that was just the beginning. Straight A's filled my report card that quarter, which was a first for me. Even my nemesis, math, didn't hold me back; now I looked forward each day to college-level algebra and accounting. Doing my best proved not only satisfying, but exhilarating, and it was all because one teacher risked being honest.

As I look back on my college days, Mr. Atkinson stands out because he refused to let me just get by. Stripping away my facade, he made me examine myself and my abilities. His red letters on my paper hit me like ice-cold water.

In the Bible, I found several instances when Jesus had to use this same type of technique. He spoke up, even when he knew his words would offend. Once with Peter, Jesus looked his friend and disciple in the eye and admonished, "Get behind me, Satan." Harsh words, but they got the message across.

God knows each of us intimately and what motivation we need. I wish gentle prodding moved me, but that doesn't always work. Sometimes I am so settled doing things my way that a rude awakening is called for.

Yep, sometimes I *need* the ugly truth.

# $C$HOSEN

JEFF ADAMS

I ALWAYS WANTED TO DO something great for God. But how could I? I never finished anything. I always gave up. I needed someone who would believe in me, even when I didn't believe in myself.

Nothing changed when I wanted to become a writer. I needed help. I joined a writers' guild. I attended critique groups. I met authors and editors at conferences. Nevertheless, three torturous years of labor produced little fruit. "God," I prayed, "how will I ever learn how to do this?"

Two years later I met Cecil Murphey at a Christian writers' conference. At our first introduction, Cec immediately stood up to embrace me. He's a hugger, not a hand shaker. A handshake isn't enough for a man who loves with his whole heart. Cec accepted me, as is.

Not many people had. In school, team captains picked me last, and only because they had to. A few years earlier at a church picnic, someone had told me I couldn't play in the softball game. Cec was different.

He is a small man with a big heart. He's written scores of books—some of them bestsellers. He speaks and teaches at conferences all over the world. Most months his calendar is full, but he's never too busy to help someone who is willing to learn.

Cec not only loves with his heart, he loves from deep within his soul. When he teaches, he is transparent. He lets you see right through his weathered exterior into his heart. With Cec, the heart of the matter is a matter of the heart. He likes others to be as open as he is.

But don't get the wrong idea. Cec is not an old softy. He's hard when it counts.

He doesn't waste words. In one critique of my work he wrote, "I stopped in the middle of the article, because I don't want to cause you more pain." When I thought my words were worthy of publication, Cec told me to "try again."

One year later, after taking his classes in yet another conference, I felt encouraged. I was learning fundamental writing skills and I'd discovered my message, but I still didn't know how to tell my story. I needed and wanted a mentor. Afraid, I never asked Cec if he would help me. I pleaded, "God, I need more help." God answered that prayer when a few weeks after the conference Cec handpicked a few students from his class, including me, to become his protégés.

He won't let me write anything but my best. He edits. He critiques. He cajoles. He challenges and pushes. He doesn't back down or let up. He tells me what I don't want to hear so I can become what I've always wanted to be.

But it's his kindness that draws me to him, the grace in his gaze, the gentle touch of hands reaching from a tender heart, the grin that wrinkles his whole face.

Some teachers write on blackboards. Others write on hearts. Cec does both. When he chose to write on my heart, his words became indelible.

That's why I love him. He chose me when I least expected it and when I had done nothing to deserve it. Our heavenly Father loves us like that.

Just when we think God can't—or won't—touch us, he stoops down from heaven and adopts us into his family. He chooses us and calls us his own.

Being chosen by Cec felt good. Being chosen by the Master Teacher feels better.

# TOUGH LOVE

## CIA CHESTER MCKOY

OUR SON FLOATED THROUGH third grade unnoticed, and we'd hoped for more involvement from his fourth-grade teacher. John Mark's three older sisters were excellent students, but we didn't know what to expect academically from our son.

The boy was two and a half when I first met him. It was his first time out of his broken crib and that dark room full of quiet children. I didn't want to be responsible for choosing the child we were meant to adopt, so I prayed that God would set affection in the right child's heart for us and not just in our hearts for him. Despite being scrawny and unused to walking on anything but a lumpy mattress, he pushed his way through a crowd of heftier gypsy children to climb up into my arms.

God answered my prayer.

John Mark was an anxious little boy from the start, eager to please and surprisingly remorseful when he did the slightest thing wrong. We adored him, but he had a hard time letting love sink in. When he started school, if he made a mistake in his work, he would call himself cruel names. To comfort him for any reason, we had to hug him from behind because he couldn't look us in the eye.

On the first day of fourth grade, the teacher was attempting to get to know her new class.

"Now I want each of you to tell me a few things about yourself to help me get to know you better. What makes you *you?* Knowing more about you should help me remember your names better."

John Mark's eyes were fixed on the ground. He could only think of two things different enough about himself to be of any interest. "I was born in Romania," he said when it was his turn, proud of his exotic heritage. Then, in full Eeyore mode, he apologized, "And I'm a C student." A funeral dirge filled his voice. It was the mournful sound of someone who had given up on ever being good enough.

A lesser teacher might have thought love should sympathize with such a pathetic child's plight. A flimsier woman might have been speechless, embarrassed for the boy. But not Miss Gehl. "Young man, look at me," she ordered.

John Mark looked up, in case she was actually speaking to him.

"You are *not* a C student. You are *becoming* an A student. Do you hear me?"

John Mark nodded like an awkward marionette whose head was being jerked up and down.

"Repeat this after me, John Mark," the surprising woman said. "'I am on my way to becoming an A student.'"

John Mark muttered the words after her under his breath.

"Say it again, this time *as if you mean it!*"

John Mark was not enjoying the attention, but he obeyed just to get out of the spotlight.

"Louder, John Mark. Say it with conviction, '*I* am becoming an *A* student!'"

It went on like that until John Mark laughed, affirming the ridiculously hopeful statement about himself with such volume that the principal across the hall peeked in the room.

By the end of the school year, John Mark's countenance and posture had transformed. He ended up making mostly As, thanks to a teacher stubborn enough to fight for the boy trapped inside a deadly perspective. This brilliant teacher refused to allow a boy's eyes to grovel when God made them to shine.

With the thought of that encounter in mind, I realized that even though I didn't spend my first two and a half years in a rundown Romanian orphanage, I too have a tendency to become easily discouraged about myself and my abilities. At times, I feel so defeated—my diabetes seems uncontrollable—and I find my shoulders drooping, just like John Mark's did that first day of fourth grade.

I turn to our God of compassion, expecting the equivalent of a sympathetic pat on the arm. I forget that God's love has a tough side, not unlike Miss Gehl's. Instead of being comforted in my slouching toward hopelessness, I get the sense that the Holy Spirit would have me fight for my health. I'd rather give up, but I know being pushed to carry on is really what I need.

When I pray for help, sure that I don't have the strength to do better, Scripture comes to mind: "I can do everything through him who gives me strength" (Philippians 4:13). Just as Miss Gehl required John Mark to repeat his affirmation about becoming an A student, I repeat God's words until they start to take root in my heart and help me overcome my weak thinking.

*True* mercy won't allow us to slide into the murkiness of depression. It's willing to be demanding, almost severe in its discipline. With the firm resolve of Master Teachers, my son and I can expect to receive the rewards promised those who stay the course and who agree with the truth that lifts *all* drooping perspectives.

# THE
# STRENGTH
## *of a*
# TEACHER

# FACING DEATH

CORRIE TEN BOOM
with Jamie Buckingham
———— from *Tramp for the Lord* ————

*If you are reproached for being Christ's followers, that is a great privilege, for
you can be sure that God's Spirit of glory is resting upon you.*
(1 PETER 4:14 PHILLIPS)

WATCHMAN NEE ONCE SAID, "When my feet were whipped
my hands suffered pain."

Christians all over the world are bound together as the body of Christ.
Many Americans, in particular, do not realize it, but a part of that body is
suffering the most terrible persecution and tribulation in the history of
mankind. If we are members of that same body—and we are—then we
must suffer with them, pray for them, and where it is possible, help them.

I remember hearing of a missionary—a single woman—who turned
her back on all her possessions at home and went to China. "Are you not
afraid?" a friend asked as she prepared to board the ship. "I am afraid of
only one thing," she said, "that I should become a grain of wheat not
willing to die."

How much more like Christ that is than the churches who gather at
Thanksgiving to sing:

Let thy congregation escape tribulation.

Several years ago I was in Africa in a little country where an enemy had taken over the government. There was great oppression against the Christians by the new government. The first night I was there some of the native Christians were commanded to come to the police station to be registered. When they arrived they were arrested and during the night they were secretly executed. The next day the same thing happened with other Christians. The third day it was the same. By that time the entire district realized that the Christians were being systematically murdered. It was the intent of the new government to eradicate them all—men, women, and children—much as Hitler tried to eradicate all the Jews.

I was to speak in a little church on Sunday morning. The people came, but I could see fear and tension written on every face. All during the service they looked at each other, their eyes asking the same questions: "Will this one I am sitting beside be the next one to be killed? Will I be the next one?"

I looked out on that congregation of black and white faces. The room was hot and stuffy. Moths and other insects came through the screenless windows and swirled around the naked light bulbs hanging over the bare, wooden benches upon which the natives sat. They were all looking at me, expecting, hoping, that I could bring them a word from God for this tragic hour.

I opened my Bible and read I Peter 4:12–14 (PHILLIPS).

And now, dear friends of mine, I beg you not to be unduly alarmed at the fiery ordeals which come to test your faith, as though this were some abnormal experience. You should be glad, because it means you are called to share Christ's sufferings. One day, when he shows himself in full splendor to men, you will be filled with the most tremendous joy. If you are reproached for being Christ's followers, that is a great privilege, for you can be sure that God's Spirit of glory is resting upon you.

I closed the Book and began to talk, simply, as an aunt would talk to her nieces and nephews. "When I was a little girl," I said, "I went to my father and said, 'Daddy, I am afraid that I will never be strong enough to be a martyr for Jesus Christ.'

" 'Tell me,' Father said, 'when you take a train trip from Haarlem to Amsterdam, when do I give you the money for the ticket? Three weeks before?'

" 'No, Daddy, you give me the money for the ticket just before we get on the train.'

" 'That is right,' my father said, 'and so it is with God's strength. Our wise Father in heaven knows when you are going to need things too. Today you do not need the strength to be a martyr; but as soon as you are called upon for the honor of facing death for Jesus, He will supply the strength you need—just in time.' "

I looked out at my African friends. Many of them had already lost loved ones to the firing squad or the headsman's axe. I knew that others would surely die that week. They were listening intently.

"I took great comfort in my father's advice," I said. "Later I had to suffer for Jesus in a concentration camp. He indeed gave me all the courage and power I needed."

My African friends were nodding seriously. They, too, believed God would supply all their needs, even the power to face death bravely.

"Tell us more, Tante Corrie," one grizzled old black man said. It was as though they were storing up all the truth they could so they could draw on it in the day of trial.

I told them of an incident that had taken place in the concentration camp at Ravensbruck. "A group of my fellow prisoners had approached me, asking me to tell them some Bible stories. In the concentration camp the guards called the Bible *das Lugenbuch*—the book of lies. Cruel death punishment had been promised for any prisoner who was found possessing a Bible or talking about the Lord. However, I went to my little cot, found my Bible, and returned to the group of prisoners.

"Suddenly I was aware of a figure behind me. One of the prisoners formed the words with her lips, 'Hide your Bible. It's Lony.' I knew Lony well. She was one of the most cruel of all the *aufseherinen*—the women guards. However, I knew that I had to obey God who had guided me so clearly to bring a Bible message to the prisoners that morning. Lony remained motionless behind me while I finished my teaching and then I said, 'Let's now sing a hymn of praise.'

"I could see the worried, anxious looks on the faces of the prisoners. Before it had been only me speaking. Now they, too, were going to have to use their mouths to sing. But I felt God wanted us to be bold, even in the face of the enemy. So—we sang.

"When the hymn was finished I heard a voice behind me. 'Another song like that one,' she said. It was Lony. She had enjoyed the singing and wanted to hear more. The prisoners took heart and we sang again—and again. Afterwards I went to her and spoke to her about the Lord Jesus Christ. Strangely, her behavior began to change until, in a crude sort of way, she became a friend."

I finished my story and stood silently while the words took their effect on my African friends. "Let me tell you what I learned from that experience," I told them. "I knew that every word I said could mean death. Yet never before had I felt such peace and joy in my heart as while I was giving the Bible message in the presence of mine enemy. God gave me the grace and power I needed—the money for the train ticket arrived just the moment I was to step on the train."

The faces before me broke into broad grins. Gone were the wrinkles of fear and anxiety. Once again their eyes were flashing with joy and their hearts were filled with peace. I closed the service by reading a poem of Amy Carmichael.

> We follow a scarred Captain,
> Should we not have scars?
> Under His faultless orders

We follow to the wars.
Lest we forget, Lord, when we meet,
Show us Thy hands and feet.

The meeting was over and the Africans stood to leave. Then softly, in the back of the room, someone began singing an old gospel song.

There's a land that is fairer than day,
And by faith we can see it afar.
For the Father waits over the way,
To prepare us a dwelling place there.
In the sweet by and by, we shall meet on that beautiful shore,
In the sweet by and by, we shall meet on that beautiful shore.

I don't know how many were killed that week, but someone told me that more than half those who had attended that service met a martyr's death—and thus received a martyr's crown. But I know that God's Spirit of glory had been resting upon them. (See I Peter 4:14.)

# FOLLOWING JESUS

JOHN WILLIAM SMITH

—— from *My Mother's Favorite Song* ——

*"If anyone would come after me, he must . . .
take up his cross and follow me."*
(MARK 8:34)

H E WAS A NINTH GRADE English teacher, and he was a Christian. He was a large man, with an athletic and intimidating physique. The school he taught in was located on the *bad side of town,* and the kids were loud, tough, crude, vulgar, and unappreciative. Although his students liked him well enough they thought he was an odd duck because he really believed that education was important and therefore took his duties much too seriously. His habit of referring to them as "Mr." or "Miss" was too much. They ridiculed him for it constantly. He told them it was a sign of respect.

It was the hardest year of teaching he had ever had, and although he had put everything he had into it, signs of progress and rewards were few. One afternoon, during the last period of a very long and difficult day, he overheard one of the boys make an extremely crude and suggestive remark to one of the girls. It wasn't that he hadn't heard it before. Maybe it was because the school had no air conditioning and he was hot, maybe it was because he had a splitting headache, maybe he was just tired and fed up—it's hard to say—

but he reacted.

"Mr. Hutchens, I am sick of your filthy mouth, I want you to stand up right now and apologize to Miss Devore."

It was quiet; Mr. Hutchens did not move. He stared at the teacher with unbelief and defiance. He had never apologized to anyone in his life, and to do so under these circumstances would be a tremendous loss of face. He remained in his seat.

"Mr. Hutchens," the teacher rose from his desk and moved to the row the boy was sitting in. His growing anger made his voice dangerously quiet—almost a whisper—and he was trembling. He was conscious of two opposing things simultaneously. First, he wished he had not made a public issue out of this, and second, he was glad he had and he didn't care. "Mr. Hutchens, I told you to stand up—and *I mean it!*"

Mr. Hutchens remained seated, glaring insolently. The teacher grabbed him by his shirt front and jerked him to his feet. The boy's legs hit his desk, and it turned over with a terrible crash, spilling books and papers everywhere. A girl in the next row bent to pick them up. "Leave them where they are, Miss Johnson. Mr. Hutchens will pick them up *after he has apologized.* Now Mr. Hutchens, I—am—waiting—for—your—apology—to—Miss—Devore, and I will not wait very long." He was spitting the words out, and his anger was out of control.

"Miss Devore?" the boy chuckled with an emphasis on the "Devore." "Don't you mean Miss De—?" He used a rhyming, common, vulgar expression for girls with loose morals. The class erupted in laughter, and he looked at the embarrassed and angry girl with an arrogant, triumphant smirk.

The teacher still had the boy's shirt grasped firmly in his left hand, and using that grip for leverage, he jerked the boy toward him and slapped him. He slapped him with every ounce of strength and energy he could muster—slapped him right across that smirking, sneering, defiant mouth. His thumb must have caught the boy's nose, or it may have simply been the tremendous impact, but the boy's nose began to bleed profusely, and there was a thin trickle of blood in the corner of his mouth.

The blow was so powerful that it stunned the boy. Angry red welts sprang to the surface of his face immediately, and he staggered and would have fallen if the teacher hadn't held him up. The only sounds in the classroom were whispers of awe and admiration from those who were impressed by the force of the blow.

The teacher's anger and resentment were quickly replaced with crushing disappointment. He marched the student, still groggy and struggling with his equilibrium, to the principal's office, seated him, explained briefly to the school secretary, and returned to his classroom. The low, excited buzz that had begun when he left was silenced at his return. He righted the desk, picked up the books and papers, and tried to return to the lesson. Fortunately, the period ended almost immediately. The students rushed into the halls to spread the news, and he went back to the principal's office to call the boy's parents and to explain in greater detail.

The principal was understanding and supportive. The boy's father came immediately, and when he heard the story, he told the teacher he wouldn't have any problems from him, that his son had gotten exactly what he deserved, and that he hoped it would teach him a lesson.

The teacher had thought it would certainly cost him his job. He knew it had already cost him something of far greater value—his self-respect and much of what he had for all these weeks been trying to teach—that Jesus makes us different. In this school, his action was much admired by the students. They spoke of the force of the blow with awe and respect in their voices—"Did you see Dick's head snap back when he hit him? It looked like he hit him with a brick." They thought more of their teacher because he had reacted *according to their standards of manhood*—"never take anything off of anybody."

He went home utterly defeated.

It came to him that night what he must do. Although there was no cafeteria, most of the kids ate sack lunches every day on the bleachers in the gym. He called the principal that night and asked him to call a school assembly the next day at noontime.

The teacher stood before a quiet, solemn student body and made a very sincere apology—not just to Mr. Hutchens, but to the faculty, the principal, and to every student whom he thought he had disappointed. He asked the forgiveness of all. When he finished, he walked toward the bleachers, his shoulders slumped, his heart heavy with failure. There was a stirring among some of the students, and from the crowd came Mr. Hutchens. He and the teacher met about half way across the floor; the boy was close to tears. They shook hands, and then the boy turned to his fellow students.

"I want to apologize to Mr. _____. What I did was wrong, and what he did was right." He paused; he was trying to work up to something, and it was tough. "I want to apologize also to Nan—Miss Devore. I'm sorry I said what I did, and I want her to forgive me." The student body stood and cheered and applauded.

The healing seemed to melt and run through the whole school. It became the "in" thing to call everybody "Mr." or "Miss." Many good-natured jokes and wisecracks came from it, but there was much goodwill too.

I wish I could say that humility always works, but it doesn't. Jesus was the most humble man who ever lived, and it got Him killed. But there is a great victory in the cross—the cross of Calvary and the cross that He has called us to bear. *There is healing and power in humility,* in foot washing, in going the extra mile, in self-sacrifice, and in turning the other cheek. Most of us never experience that healing or power because we don't have the *humility* to do those things, we're too busy—

defending our rights

*"If any man would come after me,
let him . . . take up his cross
and follow me."*

His way is never easy,
but it is always best.

# NONE MISSING

L O I S   P E C C E

WHERE'S MARGARET?" asked Mr. Elford as he checked off the attendance sheet for senior high algebra. He glanced at Margaret's best friend, Bonnie.

"She's not coming. She dropped out." All the kids knew about the grief and misery Margaret was going through with her parents' messy divorce. They sat in glum silence as Bonnie delivered the news.

Mr. Elford took in the situation. "She can't do that!" he said finally. "We're not going to let her. Where is she now?"

"Home."

"I'm going to get her."

Calling his star pupil to the front, he said, "Bryant, I'm relying on you to conduct the class. Review the homework assignment and work the problems on the board. If I'm not back in time, here is tomorrow's assignment. You know this stuff. I don't have to worry."

Bryant squared his shoulders and nodded.

Facing the rest of the class, Mr. Elford said, "I know Margaret is feeling as though she has lost her whole family. Her parents are busy with their own hurts and problems right now, and they haven't had time to help their kids work things through." He paused, giving them a significant look. "So *we* are going to be her family—everyone in this room. We're going to see that she gets to class, does her homework, keeps up with her grades, and graduates with you as she planned.

"Just one more thing besides your full cooperation: I want you to promise not to tell Margaret about this conversation."

Heads nodded eagerly.

Mr. Elford signaled Bryant to take over and headed out the door.

---

It took a while before Margaret answered the doorbell, and when she did open the door a crack she was still in her pajamas. "Wh-what are you doing here?" she stammered.

"I'm here to take you to school," said Mr. Elford.

"I'm not going back. I quit!"

"I'm not letting you quit. Your life and your future are too valuable for that."

Stunned but stubborn, she began to argue.

Mr. Elford stopped her mid-sentence. "You've got five minutes to get dressed. If you're not out here by then, I'm coming in, and I'll bring you to school in your pajamas!"

He meant it. She flew into her clothes, swiped her teeth with a toothbrush, grabbed her hairbrush, and ran downstairs to the front door: breathless, barefoot, and carrying her shoes and socks.

Wordlessly they got into the car. Halfway to the school Mr. Elford said, "Your parents are busy right now with problems that have to do with them, not you. They both love you the same as they always have. Their hopes and dreams for you haven't changed. But they are just not able at present to give you the time you need. Things will settle out soon, but meanwhile you'll be answerable to me, understand? You are going to school every day just like your parents expect you to. You'll study and do your homework. I'll be checking on you to make sure you do—and you're going to graduate with your class. What you do after graduation is up to you, but you're not going to throw your life away by dropping out. Do you hear me?"

Tears and sniffles sounded in the seat beside him and then a whispered, "Yes."

"Say it louder."

"Yes, I hear you!"

"Good. We're going to get through this thing. You'll find everybody pulling for you."

He drove into his parking space. "Math class is almost finished. Go into the girls' room and get fixed up. Stop by my room after English to pick up tomorrow's assignment."

Mr. Elford got out of his car and returned to the classroom. Margaret sat awhile and then did as he requested. Actually, she was glad to be back at school. It hurt when her parents didn't even fight her decision to quit. She had hoped it would bring them together. It did, but only to argue and blame each other for the problem. She had run crying to her room and slammed the door, but she could still hear their angry voices. That somebody like Mr. Elford cared enough to help her face responsibility left her comforted and strengthened. She dabbed her eyes with cold water, fixed her hair, and walked out of the girls' room toward her next class.

Her schoolmates kept their promise. Margaret graduated with honors the next spring. There was a tradition at graduation of reading tributes to parents and supporters and presenting them with flowers as tokens of gratitude. Margaret had been chosen to read the tributes so she was the last to pick roses out of the basket and walk into the audience to present them to her parents. They sat on opposite sides of the auditorium, emphasizing the rift between them. She went to them and gave each a rose and a hug.

With head high, she walked back to the platform with one rose in hand. Mounting the stairs, she walked across to their math teacher and class sponsor. "Mr. Elford, I'm here today because of you," she said in a clear and audible voice. She handed him the rose and gave him a quick hug while her classmates cheered and applauded.

Christ used the example of a lost sheep to illustrate the importance of each person to God. "Suppose one of you has a hundred sheep and loses one of them. Does he not leave the ninety-nine in the open country and go after the lost sheep until he finds it? And when he finds it, he joyfully puts it on his shoulders and goes home. Then he calls his friends and neighbors together and says, 'Rejoice with me; I have found my lost sheep.' I tell you that in the same way there will be more rejoicing in heaven over one sinner who repents than over ninety-nine righteous persons who do not need to repent" (Luke 15:4–7).

# THE PROVERBS 31 HOMESCHOOL MOM

JANICE THOMPSON

T HE FIRST DAY OF SCHOOL has arrived. No problem. I am
strong. I am invincible. I am a homeschool mom.

Today I begin my illustrious new career, teaching my three daughters
the three Rs, filling their heads with vast quantities of facts, and giving
them an insatiable desire for learning. Buzzing around in happy anticipation, I can hardly wait to begin the day. I am totally organized. Then I
realize what I have done. I'm teaching my three daughters. What was I
thinking? That means kids—twenty-four hours a day, seven days a week,
365 days a year.

Four days later I'm hiding in the bathroom, hands over my ears,
attempting to drown out the voice of my nine-year-old, who continues to
rap loudly on the door. Oh, not again! How did she know I would be
hiding in here?

"Mom, I don't get this!"

Megan is having a little trouble dealing with multiplication. I, on the
other hand, am having a little trouble dealing with reality.

"Just a minute, dear," I call back, turning to look at my face in the
mirror. I look pale and drawn. Maybe I've got a virus. I envision three

days' lounging in bed while the girls wait on me, hand and foot. Sounds too good to be true. No, I must admit, it's not a virus. I'm not that lucky. I'm just stressed again.

"Be anxious for nothing..." the Scripture slips through my weary mind.

"I know, I know," I say to the face in the mirror.

Sometimes things are just a little easier said than done. What I need right now is a little time alone, time to think, pray. Hiding in my bedroom is completely out of the question, since my husband works nights and sleeps during the day. Therefore, the bathroom is rapidly becoming a place of solace, a prayer closet and strategy room. But strategy must spring from creativity, and right now I can't seem to muster up any. I wander off into a daydream, trying to stall for as long as possible.

An extended period of time passes as questions roll through my mind. Whom did I think I was kidding? How could I, an ordinary mom, tackle the seemingly overwhelming job of schooling my three daughters? Only four days into the task, and I'm already wondering if I've made a mistake. Should I send them back to public school before I ruin them completely?

There is one who knows my secret fears, who knows that I can't complete this task without intervention. It's that woman in the thirty-first chapter of Proverbs, the one who gets up before dawn to prepare for her household.... The one who has her life completely together.

She scares me.

If I were to run into the Proverbs 31 lady at a Tupperware party, I would have to hide my face. I could never look the woman in the eye.

"Mom, are you still in there?" Megan's voice startles me back to reality.

"Uh, yeah."

"Don't worry about my math, Mom. I figured it out."

"You did?"

I open the door a crack and stare into her sparkling eyes.

"It's cool," she says in a very grown-up voice.

"Cool," I echo, feeling a weight lift off of me.

"You know what?"

"What, babe?"

"I've already learned more in four days than I did all last year in public school!"

"Really?" I practically shout, swinging the door open wide. "You're not just saying that? You're really learning?"

"Of course I'm learning." She laughs. "You're the best teacher I've ever had."

I take a few moments to contemplate her words. I can do this. With God's help. I need to remember not to set my sights so high that the goal is unattainable. I also need to give reality a firm handshake before I begin each day. Already I've learned that things might not go the way I've planned on paper. Interruptions, conflicts, and problems are all a part of life. But I won't let them sway me. I will not only get through this, I will succeed!

I fling the door open once more, ready to face the challenges ahead. With newfound determination and zeal, I give my daughter a warm hug. She returns it with an impish grin. Together we make our way to the classroom.

# THE LESSONS of a TEACHER

# THE TEACHING STYLE OF JESUS

DALLAS WILLARD

from *The Divine Conspiracy: Rediscovering Our Hidden Life in God*

THIS "CONCRETE" OR CONTEXTUAL method of teaching is obviously very different from how we attempt to teach and learn today, and the difference makes it difficult for us to grasp what precisely it is that Jesus is teaching. What he is saying cannot be understood unless we appreciate how he teaches, and we cannot appreciate how he teaches unless we take into account something of the world within which his teaching occurred.

We must recognize, first of all, that the aim of the popular teacher in Jesus' time was not to impart information, but to make a significant change in the lives of the hearers. Of course that may require an information transfer, but it is a peculiarly modern notion that the aim of teaching is to bring people to know things that may have no effect at all on their lives.

In our day learners usually think of themselves as containers of some sort, with a purely passive space to be filled by the information the teacher possesses and wishes to transfer—the "from jug to mug model." The teacher is to fill in empty parts of the receptacle with "truth" that may or may not later make some difference to the life of the one who has it. The teacher must get the information into them. We then "test" the patients to see if they "got it" by checking whether they can reproduce it in language rather than watching how they live.

Thus if we today were invited to hear the Sermon on the Mount—or, more likely now, the "Seminar at the Sheraton"—we would show up with notebooks, pens, and tape recorders. We would be astonished to find the disciples "just listening" to Jesus and would look around to see if someone was taping it to make sure that everyone could "get it all" if they wanted to.

Working our way through the crowd to the right-hand man, Peter, we might ask where the conference notebooks and other material were and be further astonished when he only says, "Just listen!" Perhaps we push the "record" button as we sit down, thankful that we at least will have captured all the spiritual information—if the batteries aren't dead or the tape doesn't stick.

The situation of teacher/learner was really so different in Jesus' day that we can hardly picture it to ourselves. Writing was not all that uncommon, but it was not really an option for someone trying to "get" what a teacher was saying. And then it is simply a fact that no value was placed on mere "information" as we know it today.

Of course information relevant to a real need has always been prized. But to want merely to "know stuff" such as we usually get today out of a high school and college education would have been thought laughable—if it could have been thought at all. Trivial Pursuit certainly never would have caught on as a game back then. (And a thoughtful person today might well wonder about a society in which it could catch on as the educational system is near a state of collapse. But that is another story!)

The teacher in Jesus' time—and especially the religious teacher—taught in such a way that he would impact the life flow of the hearer, leaving a lasting impression without benefit of notes, recorders, or even memorization. Whatever did not make a difference in that way just made no difference. Period. And, of course, this is true to the laws of the mind and self.

I recall with perfect clarity where I was and what I was doing when I heard that John Kennedy had been shot. My brother Duane and I were playing basketball with other students in the old gymnasium at the University of Wisconsin in Madison. We had just finished a game and were walking off the court. I remember exactly which corner of the gym and which way I was facing the instant I heard. I never wrote it down, and I never memorized it. Millions of people today can make a similar report on their own experience of this event.

We automatically remember what makes a real difference in our life. The secret of the great teacher is to speak words, to foster experiences, that impact the active flow of the hearer's life. That is what Jesus did by the way he taught. He tied his teachings to concrete events that make up the hearers' lives. He aimed his sayings at their hearts and habits as these were revealed in their daily lives.

He still takes us today in the fullness of our flight, moving right along, assuming our assumptions, and he gently but firmly lets the air out of our balloon. And as he does so, we don't have to try to "get it" and remember it. It has stuck in our life, whether we want it or agree with it or not. We will eventually have to come to terms with it somehow. The parables, the incidents, the cases where our guiding generalization about "how things are" just won't fit, sit in our minds and go off like the "tiny time capsules" of popular medications. The master teacher has done his work—or rather, keeps on doing his work.

Now, Jesus not only taught in this manner; he also taught us, his students in the kingdom, to teach in the same way. He taught about teaching in the kingdom of the heavens—using, of course, a parable. "So every bible scholar who is trained in the kingdom of the heavens is like someone over a household that shows from his treasures things new and things old" (Matt. 13:52 REV). By showing to others the presence of the kingdom in the concrete details of our shared existence, we impact the lives and hearts of our hearers, not just their heads. And they won't have to write it down to hold onto it.

# A CLEARER PICTURE

TRACIE PETERSON

—— from *The Eyes of the Heart* ——

I ONCE HAD A TEACHER give me a good lesson on perspective. I had to close my eyes, and when I opened them again, she had placed a painting up close to my face. All I could really see were splotches and blobs of color. Nothing made much sense.

She pulled the painting back just a few inches and asked me what I saw. Again, it was mostly just colors with very little detail. I told her I saw green and blue and a bit of black, maybe brown. I couldn't make out a reasonable picture; none of it made sense.

She stepped back a bit farther, and now the painting was clearer. I could make out a lake and trees. Still farther, and I found the picture widening and becoming clearer. It was a landscape, which included a cabin by the lake, and behind it were mountains and a fading sun.

The object of the lesson was to teach us about expanding our vision to take in more than what was directly in front of us. She talked of going beyond the picture, to imagine our classroom and how someone looking in from the outside would see it. Children gathered around a table. One child stood at the front of the room. The teacher held up a painting. She challenged us to keep backing up.

Take it out of the building and imagine someone with the ability to see through walls. He would see the building and the landscape around it, but would also see the room, the children, the teacher, and the painting.

We kept going, imagining our town from overhead, our state, and then our country; then the world, and finally, the entire solar system.

I remembered that object lesson because the visual was so strong. I thought a great deal about how I often see nothing more than the blotches of color in front of me. I think I know what I'm looking at; I think I have a clear picture.

Then something comes into the scene to pull me back just a bit, and suddenly I realize there is more to the situation than I thought. The eyes of your heart can look at things the same way.

At first we see God through a glass darkly. We see the Word and try to understand and comprehend our little world through God's eyes. We see the blotches and the colors—sometimes we are so close to the canvas that all we see are tiny pixels of color—so small we can't even define their hue.

In Ephesians 1:18, Paul states his hope that the eyes of your heart be enlightened that you may know the hope to which God has called you. I have that same hope for you, which is why I've written this book. All around us, God is speaking in pictures that are vivid and powerful. Sometimes we catch a glimpse, and sometimes we don't. The sad thing is, often we don't even realize that we can't see what God intends for us to see.

When my daughter Julie first started school, we had no idea she might have a vision problem. It wasn't until she was tested that we learned she had astigmatisms in each eye. I felt horrible. I didn't realize my own child was struggling to see. To her, the vision she had seemed normal. She had always seen things with those eyes—those defective eyes. She thought she had a clear picture. I thought she had a clear picture.

Maybe you think you have a clear picture of what God is trying to show you. And maybe you really do. But there's also the possibility that you're still standing with the canvas only inches away from your eyes, and God wants to show you a bigger, clearer picture.

I'll never forget when Julie got her first pair of glasses. She put them on and stood amazed at the way they changed her world. I was delighted that things came into better focus for her, but my heart nearly broke later that night when we were outside. Looking up at the sky, I heard Julie gasp.

"Oh," she said in complete delight, "the stars! I didn't know you could see them!"

She'd heard us talk about the night skies. Heard others talk about the stars in the heavens. She'd colored pictures of five-pointed stars in coloring books. But she'd never seen them with her own eyes. She didn't know it was an option.

This book is written for all the Julies out there who don't know you can see with the eyes of your heart. It's for each and every person who is still standing with his or her nose against the canvas, longing to know what the picture is.

My prayer, like Paul's, is that the eyes of your heart may be enlightened. And for what purpose? Ephesians 1:18–19 says it all: "That you may know the hope to which he has called you, the riches of his glorious inheritance in the saints, and his incomparably great power for us who believe."

There's a whole view God longs to give us. He wants to put His loving touch on your eyes and show you that He is in the picture. He longs for you to know that He is in the everyday life you live—in the tiniest details. He desires for us to have a clearer picture of who He is and who we are in Him.

Open your eyes—the eyes of your heart—and look around you. I think you're in for a pleasant surprise, but I must add a word of caution. There is a price for this kind of sight.

Once the eyes of your heart are opened, once you see God in the details and understand the bigger picture, you'll never be content to go back to having your nose on the canvas. This kind of experience will change your life—forever.

# EVEN THE LEAST OF THEM

CORRIE TEN BOOM

—— from *In My Father's House* ——

I N ADDITION TO THE WORK in the business, the club work, and the care for our children, I continued with the Bible lessons in the schools. One of these classes was for children who had learning difficulties. It was such a joy to know that the Holy Spirit doesn't need a high IQ in a person in order to reveal Himself. Even people of normal or superior intelligence need the Lord to understand the spiritual truths that are only spiritually discerned.

God gave me a great love for the "exceptional children." I remember going to these schools and telling Bible stories and being rewarded when their faces lit up with sweet and simple happiness.

Sometimes I asked them questions to see if they understood what I told them. Once a feebleminded girl answered a question of mine that might have baffled a person of normal intelligence. I asked, "What is a prophet and what is a priest?"

She said, "They are both messengers between God and man."

I continued, "Then they are the same—a prophet and a priest?"

She thought a while and then answered, "No, a prophet has his back to God and his face to us—and a priest has his face to God and his back to us."

I wasn't sure if she had learned that by heart, so I asked her, "Well, what was I today?"

She said, "You were both—you told us about God and you were a prophet. Then you prayed. You didn't pray for yourself, but you prayed for us—then you were a priest."

That was a backward child who answered in that manner! When you bring the gospel, it is the Holy Spirit who works.

I tried to teach these children other things with much less success; one time I started to instruct them about the stars. I brought some white beans to school and laid them on the table in the form of constellations. I showed them Orion, and they looked at the formation of the beans, and all of them knew it very well. Then one evening I took them outside and said, "Look, children, there is Orion . . . see it?"

They just shook their heads. "No, Tante Corrie, they are white beans in the sky."

They never understood what I told them about the stars, but the truths of the Lord they seemed to understand well.

Whenever you come in contact with feebleminded people, please tell them that Jesus loves them. They often understand God's love better than people who have problems because of their intellectual doubt.

Paul wrote in I Corinthians 1:20–21: "Where is the wise man? Where is the scribe? Where is the debater of this age? Has not God made foolish the wisdom of the world? For since in the wisdom of God the world through its wisdom did not come to know God, God was well-pleased through the foolishness of the message preached to save those who believe."

# THE STORYTELLER

JANA HEIRENDT

I WAS A TEN-YEAR-OLD girl in the fifth grade, just becoming aware of who I was and who I wanted to be. Every Thursday I watched the large school clock high on the wall with anticipation. At 10:45 she entered our classroom, and most of the class followed her across the street to a single-wide trailer for religious release time. I can close my eyes and still smell the aromatic eucalyptus trees that towered over the temporary building. I can hear my feet crunch on the carpet of bark peelings and pods that fell abundantly from those trees. Some students were excited to get out of class, but I was excited to be in her presence.

The storyteller for Child Evangelism Fellowship took her place at the front of the makeshift classroom. After praying, her hands moved to the flannelgraph. Characters from the Old and New Testaments acted out their timeless stories, as vivid as real life to my young eyes. Every Thursday, biblical truths revealed themselves to me. She spoke, but I heard the voices of Noah, King David, John, Peter, and Paul, but most of all, I heard the voice of Jesus.

Even now I have to remind myself that they were just flannel-backed cut-out figures, moved across crayon-colored backgrounds by the hand of the storyteller. Every week it happened; I felt something stir deep within me. When did she cease being the storyteller and become the presence of Jesus?

She arrived every week prepared to share another story, to smile at us, and to pray for us. She led us safely across the street to a place where we mattered, where we were respected, and where she was doing something important for our benefit. Our questions were answered with patience. She engaged our attention rather than demanded it.

Each week my anticipation grew until Thursday arrived. Glimpses of a larger world became clearer with each lesson. She always prepared a feast for my soul.

It took only one hour a week when I was ten for me to decide who I wanted to be. Her name has faded from my memory along with the details of the stories, but the truths she shared changed my life forever. The story-teller taught me how to become part of Jesus' story.

Now once a week children get off the bus to visit my makeshift class-room. I move the figures from the Old and New Testaments on the flannel-graph and watch the children's faces as the stories come to life. When is it that my smile becomes that of Jesus? Or that his voice speaks from my mouth? They may not remember my name or even the stories, but they will remember how they felt in my presence—in Jesus' presence.

# A Lesson to Remember

STEPHANIE RAY BROWN

WHEN I WALKED THROUGH the doors of Webster County High School that autumn day in 1981, I was full of anticipation and uncertainty. The anticipation was that this year I would turn that magical age of sweet sixteen.

Although most teens wanted to reach that milestone to apply for their driver's license, my wish to be sixteen was so that I could finally date my sweetheart of two years, Terry. However, along with this dream of being able to date my steady came every Webster County High School junior's misfortune of taking the dreaded requirement of United States history.

Since my elementary school years, I had heard nightmare accounts of teacher Hugh Ridenour and his huge expectations for his students. As I entered his classroom, my heart began to beat rapidly. I felt like a defendant about to be sentenced in a courtroom.

As the weeks and months passed, Mr. Ridenour's academic standards were all I had heard they would be. I had to adjust to his method of evaluation. This was my first experience with essay tests and with class participation being a good percentage of the grade for this course.

At Christmas, I was so proud to average an A for the semester.

However, in February, my world fell apart when Terry and I broke up. My grade quickly fell from an A to a C. I wasn't surprised when Mr. Ridenour called me in for a conference. But I was terrified.

Expecting to hear a sermon about doing my best or even a "there are other fish in the sea" speech, this icon of a teacher surprised me. Although his discussion began with his disappointment over my grade drop, Mr. Ridenour said that he understood the reason. He shared his feelings about when his heart had been broken. He also told me that there was something besides the grade drop that troubled him about me.

"No matter how much you love someone, you should never quit loving yourself," he stated. "Have that confidence in yourself that you eagerly place in someone else. If you do not believe in yourself, who will?"

As I left his room, I continued to evaluate his words and wondered what I was to do with my future. That weekend I did some serious praying. As I read my Bible, I was reminded of how much God loved me. If God loved me, I must be special and should love me too.

On that Monday, I prayed for strength to get through the day without falling apart when I saw Terry. That afternoon Terry met me at my locker and asked if he could call me. "Sure," I said nonchalantly, thinking he just wanted to talk as a friend.

His phone call was the first step in our reconciliation. After much prayer for the ability to forgive and forget, Terry and I dated throughout my high school as well as college days. I graduated from Murray State a week before our wedding. After college, when I achieved my lifelong dream of becoming a teacher, I never forgot Mr. Ridenour or his wonderful words.

As a teacher I expect high standards from my students. I also try to show my concern and compassion. I want them to know that in order to be loved and respected one must love as well as believe in themselves first. God wants us to. The golden rule says to love others as you love yourself. This lesson had been taught well by Mr. Ridenour. I also try to remember it when life—like being sixteen—is not always sweet.

# $\mathcal{T}$HE WATER PITCHER: LEARNING THE WHOLE BIBLE

ELMER L. TOWNS

~ from *Stories on the Front Porch* ~

T HE FIRST SUNDAY I was in his class he hunkered down over the stainless steel table [in the church kitchen, our classroom] and announced, "I'm gonna teach you the WHOLE BIBLE."

*Wow!* I responded inwardly. *The WHOLE BIBLE.*

The Bible was a mysterious black book I saw in our home and in the home of all my aunts and uncles. People spoke with reverence about the Bible. "Don't *ever* put anything on top of a Bible," I was told.

Now here Jimmy Breland was saying, "I'm gonna teach you the WHOLE BIBLE from cover to cover."

Some critics today might cringe at the idea of any Bible teacher making such a claim, especially someone like Jimmy Breland who had only an eighth-grade education. But Breland could excite young minds. He could electrify dreams; and he taught his juniors "the WHOLE BIBLE."

Breland did not lecture. He did not give speeches. When he opened his mouth, enthusiasm flowed. It would have been obvious even to a casual observer that he was excited about what he knew. He was a storyteller, and his junior boys and girls stepped into the world of his story. He didn't just tell stories about Abraham; he made Abraham live. When he told how Abraham obeyed God, I wanted to obey God. When he told about Abraham's lie about his wife Sarah, the class cringed with guilt.

Breland was not schooled in the use of Greek, Hebrew or biblical exegesis, but he was remarkably fluent in the language generally understood by kids growing up in Savannah, Georgia.

## ABRAHAM, WHO BEGAN IT ALL

"Abraham was a scalawag!" Breland declared. People in my hometown knew that a scalawag was a mischievous boy dabbling in devilment. A scalawag was not an evil boy, but an average boy who liked to tease and play, and who didn't always obey. Mischievous little boys who got into devilment from time to time were scalawags; and I was a scalawag, just like Abraham.

When Breland caught someone not paying attention, he reached up among the utensils above his head and grabbed an old aluminum water pitcher. He didn't have the sort of visual aids publishers provide for Sunday school teachers today, so he used a water pitcher.

"This pitcher is Abraham, who began it all," he announced, holding up the dented pitcher.

Twenty-four pairs of eyes focused on that dented pitcher. He waved it high above our eyes, and everyone kept watching. "This is Abraham, who began it all."

Maybe because he was a Presbyterian, Jimmy Breland always described Abraham as the one "who began it all." He was no doubt aware that Adam was the first man, so in a way, of course, Adam began it all. To some "Covenant Presbyterians," however, the covenant of grace is dated from God's covenant with Abraham.

"Who is the water pitcher?" Jimmy asked a boy not paying attention.

He always focused on students not focused on him.

"Abraham," the boy answered. That wasn't the answer Jimmy wanted from the student. Jimmy wanted a complete answer.

"Abraham, who began it all," Jimmy Breland added. "God poured His grace into Abraham." The effect was captivating as he walked over to the sink and filled the pitcher with water. "God poured His grace into Abraham so Abraham could be emptied onto the world."

Even the greatest Sunday school teachers in the world have moments when they encounter difficulty captivating the attention of every pupil. Whenever Jimmy Breland lost our attention, he did what good teachers always do to regain it. He asked a question.

"Who is the water pitcher?" he asked, waving the pitcher in front of the boy whose thoughts had begun to wander.

"Uh … uh …" the boy stammered. "The water pitcher who began it all."

The answer was close enough to win a smile from Jimmy Breland as he corrected, *"Abraham,* who began it all."

The next week in Sunday School was more of the same. Jimmy Breland began the class by holding up the water pitcher and asking, "Who is this?"

"Abraham, who began it all," the class cried in unison.

"Aw, you can do better than that," Breland coaxed. And better we did as we hollered, "ABRAHAM, WHO BEGAN IT ALL."

## THE SINS OF THE FATHERS

"This is Isaac," Breland continued, as he reached for the sugar bowl. "This week's lesson is about the son of Abraham."

That day the class heard the story of Isaac's birth to the 100-year-old "Abraham, who began it all." Whenever he lost eye contact with his students, Jimmy Breland rescued it with a question. "Who is the water pitcher?" Sometimes he asked, "Who is the sugar bowl?"

The next week he added, "Who are the salt and pepper shakers?" He held them high as he walked back and forth in front of the class. The salt and pepper shakers, we learned, were Jacob and Esau respectively, the sons of Isaac. Breland explained how Abraham lied, next Isaac lied, but the biggest liar of them all was Jacob. From behind the food preparation counter in the kitchen of Eastern Heights Presbyterian Church, this master teacher soberly announced, "The sins of the father are passed on to the son."

The thought terrified me. The greatest sin of my father was drunkenness—at least that is what I thought was the greatest sin. The senior Towns was a good man who loved his children, but alcohol was beginning to destroy his life. He was not just a closet drunk. Everyone in the neighborhood had seen him staggering home. I could remember the times I had been sent out into the street to help my drunken father get up from the dirt street and lumber into the house. Neighbors sat on their porches laughing at the man floundering in the dirt. I was embarrassed, and I cried as I helped my drunken father home. Then when we finally got into the house, my mother's yelling could be heard several houses away.

Of course I did not want the sins of my father passed along to me. So I reasoned in Sunday school class: *I don't want to be a drunk like my father.* Perhaps there in the kitchen of Eastern Heights Presbyterian Church where Jimmy Breland taught about the sins of the fathers is where I determined never to take my first drink of whiskey. This commitment was strictly kept for the rest of my life.

## REVIEW TIME

"Let's review," Breland said each week. He began the class by holding up the various utensils from the kitchen. There was the water pitcher, the sugar bowl, salt and pepper shakers, a butcher knife, the knife sharpener, the potato peeler and even a Coca-Cola glass. The list seemed as endless as the Old Testament itself. We always took great delight in helping Jimmy Breland remember the utensils he forgot.

Occasionally he teased us. He held up the meat cleaver for the 400 years in Egypt, but we all knew it represented the 400 years of the Judges—the knife sharpener represented the 400 years in Egypt.

Nonetheless, Breland taught us "the WHOLE BIBLE." He included the prophets such as Obadiah, Micah and Zephaniah, putting them in their proper chronological sequence among the kings. We learned what each prophet did and how he fit into the historic sequence of God's plan. Week by week, the faded yellow walls of the kitchen in the Eastern Heights Presbyterian Church witnessed an odyssey of supernatural proportions.

Lives were being changed.

I remember the day Jimmy Breland began the class with a review that started with Abraham and marched through all the Old Testament books. He lined up the kitchen utensils on the edge of the stainless steel table, one after the other. We kids shouted out the biblical character as Jimmy Breland held up a utensil. The butcher knife divided the kingdom of Solomon into the tribes of Israel to the north and Judah to the south. Some in the class could repeat from memory the kings of Judah. Then we came to the postexilic books—Ezra, Nehemiah and Esther. We covered those, too. And that was the end of the Old Testament.

## JOB, AS IN "ROBE"

"Do you know who this is?" Jimmy Breland asked, holding up a Coca-Cola glass.

"No," we said in unison, shaking our heads.

"The Coca-Cola glass is the next book in the Bible," Jimmy Breland said, smiling. We began to thumb intently throughout the Old Testament to find the book that followed Esther. I found it, but didn't call out.

"Elmer?" Breland said, seeing that I had found the place in my Bible. "Who is the Coca-Cola glass?"

"Job," I said, pronouncing the name like a working "job" a person is paid to do.

"No it's *Job*," Jimmy Breland corrected me, pronouncing the o as in "robe."

I did not want to be disrespectful, but I had to come back with, "Looks like Job to me," again pronouncing it like "job."

The class laughed. Jimmy Breland ignored me and took the Coca-Cola glass and asked dramatically, "Where does Job fit on the table?"

We shook our heads back and forth, for we didn't know. Jimmy Breland held up the Coke glass over the kings and said, "He doesn't go here." Then he held Job over the times of the judges and noted, "Doesn't go here." He walked slowly, dramatically, quietly down the line of kitchen utensils and finally put the glass next to the water pitcher and announced, "Job and Abraham were contemporaries."

I didn't know what that meant, and I'm not sure anyone else in the room knew. Jimmy must have sensed our frustration, for he then said, "If Job and Abraham were little boys, they would have played together." We all understood that.

That survey of the Old Testament has stuck with me through the years. I have taught a Historical Survey of the Old Testament to university students and written a textbook about the topic. The best Bible survey I have ever had of the WHOLE BIBLE, however, was with Jimmy Breland, who started his class with a dented water pitcher and "Abraham, who began it all."

## COMMUNICATING LASTING LESSONS

According to an early count, 19 of the 24 of us children in Jimmy Breland's class went into Christian ministry. Dr. Albert Freundt became the distinguished professor of church history at Reformed Presbyterian Seminary in Jackson, Mississippi. Others became pastors, missionaries and Christian school teachers, and I became a college president.

Once I was having lunch with Dr. Frank Perry, another product of Jimmy Breland's class, who grew up to be pastor of a 1,400-member Southern Baptist church on the north side of Atlanta. Knowing of my love for college teaching, he asked, "Who was the greatest teacher you ever had?"

I suspected the question was not straightforward, and he had an ulterior motive. "What are you getting at?" I asked. Dr. Perry told me he was trying to determine why so many of us from Eastern Heights Presbyterian Church went into full-time Christian service.

"Jimmy Breland," I replied immediately.

Then Dr. Perry looked at me and asked, "Who was the spatula?" We laughed as friends do when they know the answer to a question that bonds them together.

Jimmy Breland's love of the Bible became my love. He communicated passion and dreams. He made God's Word live. He had very little to work with, just average boys and girls from average homes. His classroom was not conducive to teaching and contained no educational furniture or equipment. He had an eighth-grade education. Yet his teaching electrified his students and I learned the WHOLE BIBLE.

SECTION SIX

# THE
# PROVISION
## of a
# TEACHER

# THE BOY
# NOBODY LOVED

PATRICIA S. LAYE

"TOMMY IS THE MEANEST child I've ever seen," I commented to my best friend, the principal. I was the school social worker and knew this child well.

Tommy had kicked a smaller boy in the leg as they stood waiting their turn at the water fountain. The injured child cried out and clutched his knee, yelling, "Miss Jones, Miss Jones, Tommy kicked me again."

The principal frowned and stepped forward. "I saw the incident. I'll take Tommy with me." Putting her arm on Tommy's shoulder, she marched him off to her office, a place he was as familiar with as his classroom. His classmates giggled at the fate that lay in store for Tommy. Without a flicker of fear or a shred of remorse, Tommy walked silently down the hall.

When school ended that day, I still had Tommy on my mind, so I stopped by the principal's office. "How did you punish Tommy this time?" I asked and sat down.

My friend stood and closed her office door so we wouldn't be overheard. She shook her head sadly. "I gave him three days in after-school suspension."

"Do you think it will help?"

"No, I don't." Her determination registered in her voice as she said, "I'm going to save him though."

"Good luck. I don't want to discourage you, but Tommy shows all the characteristics of a child headed for serious trouble if he doesn't turn his life around." I'd seen too many Tommys in my career.

Maybe I was too jaded for the job any longer, yet I loved children too much to quit. It bothered me every time I saw a child in as much pain as Tommy, but to date I had not been able to touch his heart or help him.

"Tell me about him," my friend said. "I want to know about his home life, his church affiliation, his siblings and parents."

Memories of my experiences with Tommy's family and his home environment filled me with a sense of failure. I said, "It's as sad a case as you'll find. His father is an alcoholic. His mother works and struggles to support the family as best she can. Both parents lack the education needed to earn more than minimum wages. The house is filthy. You've noticed that Tommy is never clean."

"Yes. One of the reasons he's angry is that he smells and looks dirty, so people make fun of him." The principal shook her head. "But that's not all that is wrong with Tommy. He needs God in his life. I asked him if he went to Sunday school. He said that he didn't. Some church needs to offer a hand to that family."

"They have. The mother says that she and the children don't have the proper clothes to wear. A Sunday school class bought them clothes. That didn't work. The mother always overslept and didn't have the children ready when the church bus came to pick them up. The father said that he had no use or respect for churches, preachers, or do-gooders, as he called the people who offered help."

"Then I'll just have to start with Tommy and teach him about Jesus myself."

"You know the state forbids the teaching of religion in school. You may get in trouble."

"When has the state saved a man in prison? Jesus saves criminals by showing them God's way of living is better. I'm going to find the good in Tommy and work with that before all the kindness and loving has been destroyed in his heart." She stood and walked to the door. "My mind is made up. Tommy is already on probation for stealing. I'm going to turn this young man around before he gets into serious trouble."

My friend's determination to disobey the school board's policy concerned me. She was an excellent principal. "What you're planning to do is admirable, but I'd hate to see you lose your job."

"If the board fires me, you can add me to your soup kitchen list."

In the following weeks I watched as my friend worked with that twelve-year-old boy. The first outward change I saw in him was his appearance. But he was still the class bully and didn't have any friends. Then one day I passed him in the hall, he glanced up at me, and gave me the most beautiful smile.

"Hello, Tommy, how are you doing in school?"

The smile faded and his blue eyes clouded. I realized I'd said the wrong thing. So, noticing the clean blue plaid shirt he wore, I said, "That certainly is a pretty shirt you're wearing. You look like you've grown two inches."

The grin returned and he ran his hand down his side. "These are new jeans too."

"You look very nice. Keep up the good work." I patted him on the shoulder and watched him walk down the hall with pride in his step.

Later that day I stopped by the principal's office. "How are you coming along with your project? I noticed how nice he looked today. He was actually smiling."

"It's a hard fight," she said, "but I think I see a little progress."

"I hope you don't go broke buying him new clothes." I thought of all the times Tommy's family had received clothes and gifts in the past. "The last time the church gave him clothes after they got filthy he let the dogs sleep on them on the front porch."

"I took him to the washroom near the gym and taught him how to wash his own clothes in the washing machine. His mother has one, but nobody uses it much. I bought him a large box of washing powder that he keeps in his bedroom. When it runs out, I told him I'd buy more." She grinned. "Do you know that he hasn't worn dirty clothes to school since that day? I've noticed his little sisters' clothes seem cleaner too." She remained silent for a minute before continuing. "Now it's time to clean up his soul. There is so much anger there. I pray nightly for him. Will you do the same?"

"Of course I will."

"He comes to my office early every morning before the other students arrive. We've started having morning devotionals together."

My surprise showed. Was this the same Tommy who used to be late nearly every morning? Driving from one school to another, I had picked Tommy up many mornings lagging to school long after the tardy bell had rung. "I'm impressed."

"Can you believe he didn't know any of the stories about Jesus? He's a lot brighter than I thought, though. He asks interesting questions."

That year ended, and the following school term I searched for Tommy in the halls, curious to see how my friend's project was coming along. To my dismay I encountered Tommy's new teacher leading him by the arm, dragging him toward the office. His clothes were as dirty as ever. This time he had a bloody nose and was sobbing quietly, wiping his runny nose on his soiled and ragged shirt.

After school the principal came to my office. "I suppose you heard about Tommy's terrible fight today?" She looked crestfallen.

"He seems to have reverted back to his old ways."

Sitting down beside me, she picked up the worn Bible I kept in my bookcase and thumbed through it. "I have prayed for God to show me the way to save Tommy. He wants to be a good person. He really does. It just seems the devil undoes everything he accomplishes." Shutting the Bible, she said, "You know his father stopped him from washing his clothes and forbade him to attend church, don't you?"

"No," I said, shocked that the man could be so cruel. "I can stop that.

I'll go to the Department of Family and Children Services. The caseworker and I will call in the parents. We'll let that man know in no uncertain terms that Tommy can and will wash his clothes and his siblings' clothes as needed. Tommy will attend church, if that's his desire. That much I can help you with."

"What if the father takes it out on Tommy and beats him? That's what he did last summer." She dabbed at her eyes. "Poor Tommy. How can he keep living and surviving in such an environment?" She shook her head. "Tommy was embarrassed to tell me what had happened. He told me that he'd prayed to Jesus to make his daddy stop drinking, and to be kind to his mother and them, but that Jesus had let him down." She had tears in her eyes. "How do I explain to him that Jesus loves him and all things will work out for the good in the end?"

"Let's keep praying for Tommy. In the meantime I'll see what the state can do with Tommy's father. The mother seems to care but is too scared of the father to stand up to him."

Within a few weeks Tommy was coming to school clean and behaving much better again. For his birthday the principal gave him a Bible with his name printed on it in gold. His grades improved and he graduated from middle school and went on to the high school. The family eventually moved away and I lost contact with him. When I saw a troubled little boy, memories of Tommy surfaced. I often wondered where he was and if his life had continued to improve.

Years later our minister announced the name of the preacher selected to lead our revival. Could he possibly mean the Tommy I remembered, or was the name merely a coincidence? I could hardly wait for the first night of services.

A handsome man, with a pretty wife and three lovely children, stood and began the service. It *was* Tommy. He retold the story of how a teacher had saved his life and his soul when all the churches and many others had given up on him. He also told how the Bible he held up for us to see was the one given to him by that teacher years ago. "I own a dozen different

Bibles in various versions, but none means as much to me as this one. This is the one that saved me."

He continued to tell the hushed congregation the story of his life. He told how he learned to forgive his father, and how he applied the same determination the teacher did to him to save his drunken father. Before his father's death, the parent professed his belief in God and joined the church. "Today I would likely be in prison, if not for one teacher caring. Just like Jesus, she forgave and forgave. Not once did she give up on me. By example we touch others."

Tommy's words brought tears to my eyes as I bowed my head to say a silent prayer. "God, please never let me give up on a child again. The boy nobody loved has shown me the power of love. Your teachings have proven the healing rewards of faith. May I never forget either again."

# $\mathcal{T}$IM'S CHALLENGE

B A R B A R A    J O H N S O N

⎯ from *Where Does a Mother Go to Resign?* ⎯

T HERE'S SOMETHING SO extra-special about your firstborn child, and our twenty-three-year-old Tim was frequently in my thoughts. I sensed that he was restless, almost as though he were running from something—perhaps an emptiness in his life. He had graduated recently from the Los Angeles Police Academy and, while he didn't have any earthshaking problems, Tim felt within himself the need for some kind of new challenge.

So it was in that summer of 1973 that Tim and two friends decided to take off in a little blue Volkswagen "Bug" for a summer in Alaska. Al was eager to escape the pressures of college exams; and Ron, also twenty-three, was trying to run from a more serious responsibility—a rapidly dissolving marriage.

They were off on a new adventure—to make some money and see our country's last frontier.

After nearly two weeks of hard driving and failure to find work to sustain their venture, not only was their morale deflated but so were their wallets. Even the "work wanted" ad scrawled in the dust caking the side of their VW hadn't helped.

Resigned to the fact that they'd about reached the limit of their resources, and hoping they'd have enough cash to make it home to Southern California, the three pulled into an Anchorage gas station to fill up the tank for the beginning of the long trip back home.

Little did they know that this gas stop was to change their lives. They had no way of knowing that Ted McReynolds, a resourceful school teacher who pumps gas in the summer, specialized all year round in showering people with his Christian love and concern.

Ted has the knack of being in the right place at the right time. That's where he was the day our three weary travelers pulled into the service station. Ted read the dusty printing on the side of the car: "We are Al, Tim and Ron from California. We need work." And he also read the messages in the boys' faces. He perceived that their need was much deeper than finding employment. So while their VW was being serviced, he talked to them about Jesus.

None of the young men were committed Christians. Tim, although surrounded by Christianity, remained very "ho hum" about his faith. Like many youngsters, he had waded through Sunday school, memory verses, and even attendance at a Christian day school. He had invited Christ into his life some six months prior to their trip (after talking to a friend who shared "The Four Spiritual Laws" with him), and on the following day, Tim had led Ron to make the same decision. Neither, however, had really gotten a handle on what was meant by the Christian walk, a daily fellowship experience with the living Christ.

After talking to them about Jesus, Ted invited all three boys to come home with him for dinner. They were reluctant, but accepted after Tim reminded the other two of the first rule of the road: "Never turn down a free meal!" They planned to stay one meal, but ended up staying five weeks!

The hospitality and the spiritual nourishment offered by the McReynoldses met a real need in their lives. Although Tim and Ron had made a profession of faith, they were starved spiritually for this nourishment they were receiving. Life began to take on a whole new meaning for them, and then Al, too, made a commitment of his life to Jesus.

The boys held late night rap sessions with Ted and began to share their faith with others. They joined in the fellowship at the Abbott Loop Chapel where they could sense the presence of God's love and goodness in the lives of the believers.

Ted assisted in securing construction jobs for them to earn enough money to get home. The rewards of a hard day's physical labor for a good wage were secondary, however, when contrasted with the good things of God they were receiving.

After two months, Ron and Tim felt ready to leave for California. They were eager to see their families. Tim wrote in one of his letters to us: "This trip has been fantastic.... I had a chance to do a lot of 'deep thinking' about myself.... I get so excited about all the wonderful things— burdens lifted, peace of mind.... It's beautiful.... No more worries or cares—what can I say but *it's fabulous!!*"

And Ron wrote to his family: "I just can't explain how happy I am.... I cannot tell you how much my life has changed. I want to come home and explain it better.... I want you to receive Christ into your hearts."

When we read Tim's letters, we didn't know quite what to think. His statements came across with such emotion, such *zing!* He seemed so excited, so thrilled. I can remember telling myself, "Whatever it is, even if this lasts only for a flash—great!" I was having real trouble adjusting to this new image. Our son who left for Alaska because he had become disenchanted with his work and a bit disillusioned with life in general was the more familiar one. Although Tim said he was a Christian, I had never seen him really "plugged in," never seen him in the swim—he had merely been dog-paddling along or treading water when it came to his Christian experience.

––––––––––

*Editor's Note: The teacher heart of Ted McReynolds continued to give even during summer* vacation. He had no way of knowing the impact he would have on the lives of three young men who were far from home—both their earthly homes and their spiritual home. What Ted McReynolds provided for those boys that summer was more than just jobs and housing. His provisions included life lessons with eternal consequences. Ted had no way of knowing the future, but his influence would be the saving grace for both Tim and Ron, who died in a head-on collision with a truck during their trip home.

# AN ACT OF LEGISLATURE

JOY CLARY BROWN

N OTHING CAN BE DONE. It's state law.

"I'm sorry, Mrs. Brown. I don't know how to tell you this, but Alex missed passing the exit exam by one point because of 'awkward word usage.'"

The words weighed heavy in my heart and mind. Eventually, those same words would prompt a three-day miracle this teacher will never forget.

As the itinerant teacher for hearing disabled in our county, I had worked every day with Alex the four years he attended high school. Profoundly deaf from birth, he was an amazing young man. He had maintained a B average in his college preparatory classes, including two years of a foreign language.

In order to graduate from high school with a diploma, students were required to pass an exit exam. The exam was given annually beginning in the sophomore year.

Alex passed all areas of the exam the first year he took it, except the area of written expression. Three years in a row, he failed that portion by one point with the same explanation attached, "awkward word usage."

"Awkward word usage" is a common challenge for deaf and foreign students. When English is a second language, verb tenses especially are affected.

Repeatedly I called and wrote the State Department of Education encouraging them to consider the special needs of deaf and foreign students when grading the written expression portion of the exit exam. The same reply was given consistently, "Nothing can be done. It's state law."

Students who had failed portions of the exam were allowed by state law to take it twice their senior year, once before Christmas break and again at the end of the school year. Alex diligently prepared for the exam, writing voluminously for practice. He took the first-semester exam. When his grade arrived he had missed passing by one point with the all-too-familiar phrase attached, "awkward word usage."

Now Alex had only one more chance, the spring semester exam. After four more months of intense coaching, I felt confident he was adequately prepared. He took the exam for the final time and we anxiously awaited the results. Friday morning, two weeks before graduation, his principal called me into the office to inform me of the exam score. Reluctantly he said, "I'm sorry, Mrs. Brown. I don't know how to tell you this, but Alex missed passing the exit exam by one point because of 'awkward word usage.'"

Hot tears stung my face as I apologetically replied, "I'm sorry. I know this is not very professional, but you know he deserves a diploma." The principal called the guidance counselor into the room. Upon hearing the news, she also began to cry. We had witnessed how hard this young man tried. We had watched as he struggled to excel.

"Have you told his parents?" I asked after I was composed enough to talk.

"No," the principal solemnly replied.

Not quite sure why I was asking, I requested that he wait until after the weekend to tell them. I left Alex's school in a daze. As I traveled across the country roads to my next school, the tears were flowing so freely I could hardly see to drive.

Suddenly, as though looking through a prism, I noticed the lush farmland along the side of the road. The beauty of the verdant fields reminded me of the majesty of God. Talking to myself I said aloud, "You serve a just God. What has happened to Alex is not just. God cares about the Alexes of the world."

Then, as though hearing a tape recording in my mind, the words echoed, "Nothing can be done. It's state law." At that point I determined, "The law needs to be changed."

After traveling to visit my parents that evening, I called my sister, who was in college pursuing a degree in education, and asked her to bring her educational law textbooks to our parents' home. I explained, "We have to find a loophole in there somewhere."

After hours of poring over the pages of the texts, my eyes fell upon the words for which we had been searching. "Here it is! There is a federal law against culturally biased testing. Since English is a second language for deaf and foreign students, to grade their written expressions the same as hearing, English-speaking students is culturally biased!"

My sister and I leaped to our feet, hugging each other as we celebrated.

Our father, who was a quiet man, smiled while observing the joyous scene. Then he inquired, "Did you know Olin is on the House Educational Committee?"

"What?" I exclaimed. "I knew he was in the House of Representatives, but I didn't know he was on that committee."

Olin Phillips had been a friend of the family for many years. I immediately tried to reach him, but he was out of town. After trying for the next few days, I was able to speak with him late Monday evening. "Olin, you know I would not bother you if it were not important."

He thoughtfully listened to the situation and responded, "It sounds to me like that law needs to be changed."

"Exactly," I agreed.

"I will get back to you," Olin assured.

We were less than two weeks from graduation. I reasoned that Alex would have to graduate with a certificate rather than a diploma. He could enroll in adult education for a year, and maybe by the next spring a more fair law would be passed and he could receive his diploma.

Then, Thursday night, one week before graduation, Olin called our home. "Here is what's happening. A senator from another county introduced a bill to exempt foreign students from the written expression portion of the exit exam until an alternative assessment could be taken under consideration. It has been stuck in Senate committee for a month. Our only hope is to get it out of the Senate committee to the floor.

"In order for a bill to become a law it has to go through three separate readings on three separate days and the governor can take up to two weeks to sign it. We are in session three days next week, and then we recess until January.

"Our only hope is to put pressure on the Senate to bring it out of committee. Then we must get it amended to include the deaf, get the House to concur with the Senate amendment, and get it through the three readings on our final three days in session."

"Olin," I asked, "Are you saying we have a chance to get the law changed this school year before graduation?"

"Yes, but it's a long shot," he said.

I hung up the phone and smiled. "God does care about the Alexes of the world."

The next day Alex's principal and I drafted a letter praising Alex as a student. The entire faculty signed it. I made copies of the federal law against culturally biased testing, as well as the correspondence from the State Department of Education stating, "Nothing can be done. It's state law." We started getting packets to the offices of Senate and House members. Alex's parents and I called many of them at home. The weekend was a flurry of activities as we began putting pressure on our state legislators.

On Monday morning, as I arrived at one of my schools, the principal called me into his office and said that I had a message to call Olin on the floor of the House of Representatives. With a shaky finger I dialed the number and heard his happy voice answer, "We got it out of Senate committee, amended to include the deaf, and we got it through the first reading!"

Tuesday came. Again, the happy voice of this well-respected man announced, "The House concurred with the Senate amendment, and I got it through the second reading. I've alerted the governor that this bill might pass as a law, and he has agreed to sign it on the spot if it does. Call me at this number tomorrow and I'll give you the final update."

On Wednesday a room full of administrators and teachers gathered around the phone as I placed the call. The voice on the other end assured me, "I'm trying hard, but we are being bombarded since we are in closing sessions."

When I arrived home, my husband gave the good news. Olin had called. The law had passed. Two days later, on Friday night, a young deaf man named Alex walked across the stage of his high school auditorium and received a much-deserved diploma.

Through this experience I learned a valuable lesson. Even though I as a teacher cared deeply about the situation, the Great Teacher cared even more. Life may be difficult at times, but he cares about everything that concerns us, and he cares about the Alexes of the world.

# EXPERIMENTAL LESSONS

T W I L A   S I A S

S URELY SHE WAS NOT as tall as I remember. The impression of
height may have been because she always stood in that polite, regal
manner—head erect and back straight. She wore her black hair pulled back
gracefully, often in a tight French roll. Long, articulate fingers stretched
from strong-looking hands, capable of demonstrating the technical aspects
of even the daintiest trill in a Mozart piece.

Mrs. Catherine Casey was my piano teacher for twelve years, from first
grade through high school. A marvelously popular teacher, she typically
taught sixty to seventy students each week. The year-end recitals were all-
out marathons, sometimes lasting more than four hours. Student render-
ings ranged everywhere from "Birthday Party" out of John Thompson's
beginner's book, right up to the challenging Rachmaninoff concertos.

But she was more than just a piano teacher. Her beautiful home, out
in the country on a gravel road, was a haven. My lessons were on Tuesdays,
immediately after school. In fact, I had special permission to ride the bus
route that would drop me off at her door for my lesson time. On snowy
days, the fireplace hosted a warm, crackling fire, and Mrs. Casey served hot

cocoa in fragile china cups, with "boughten" cookies on a matching, equally delicate plate.

In many ways, she seemed a rare, brilliant flower in a garden of the usual assortment of lovely plants. She had a classy sophistication about her in an area where people were generally countrified in manner. Most of her relatives were members of the local A.M.E. church—the African Methodist Episcopal. She, however, preferred the formal liturgy and music of the St. Lawrence Catholic Church in town. Still, she was never pretentious.

Her formal musical training had taken her to a conservatory, where she had completed all the course work but had not been officially granted a degree. Not granting degrees to people with her skin color was apparently a common practice back when Catherine Casey had gone to the city for her professional education.

As a child, I was unaware of those types of injustices. I did notice that our hands playing duets together were shaded a bit differently, but I was more focused on trying to make my hands look and move just like hers—gliding, attacking, phrasing, and resting with the rounded, invisible bubble in the palm.

The most significant occurrence with that remarkable teacher took place the day we met. My mom and dad had a strong conviction that I should learn to play the piano, and in typical five-year-old style, I swept right along in the wake of their enthusiasm for piano lessons. After having called for an appointment, Dad drove me to Mrs. Casey's home to arrange for lessons.

Her warmth quickly drew me in as I eagerly expressed my desire for music. I wandered over to the side of the sofa and began looking through her stack of *Ebony* magazines. A few feet away, Mrs. Casey and Dad discussed the financial details. I noted a concerned look on his face. Even at that innocent age, I was aware that our family had little money for any extras.

Mrs. Casey's overall dignity included a precise, formal speaking manner, but her voice remained gentle as she made the proposal to my dad: "I have recently been researching some new methods for piano instruction. Now, since these techniques are new to me and are not yet proven successful, I was wondering if you might consider letting Twila become my student, sort of on an experimental level, so that I might have an opportunity to test this new system of instruction. Now, I would certainly not feel right about charging the regular fee for my services. You would be doing me a favor, and the lesson costs would be significantly reduced."

The look on Dad's face was a mixture of humility and gratitude. It seems Mrs. Casey had enough dignity and grace to go around for everyone. Dad accepted her generous offer, and I wondered what strange, new methods would face me at weekly lessons. Year after year, I studied with her at a reduced rate. Occasionally, the regular rates would go up, and my lesson fees would rise, as well. All through high school, my lessons continued to be possible because of the adjusted fee.

Sometimes I'm a bit slow to catch on. After nearly twelve years of lessons and watching other children during their lessons, I realized that there were no special "experimental" methods of instruction. I was obviously being taught just like everyone else. I finally asked Mom about the arrangement of reduced fees for experimental instruction. Mom smiled as she explained.

My folks were aware that Mrs. Casey's godly and generous heart was matched with her desire to save the pride and dignity of a rather poor family. She believed—and rightly so—that my folks couldn't afford the regular lesson price. She also was certain that they wouldn't accept a reduced rate under normal circumstances, so she came up with the offering of the special arrangement—which at first had seemed plausible to my folks. After a while, they were on to her. But they realized it was the only way I would ever have lessons. And Catherine Casey seemed eager to give the gift.

Amazing—the generosity of someone from whom so much had been withheld. She shared her classic style and grace with hundreds of students during her life. What I have forever taken with me is the heart of a great teacher—love and sacrifice.

The passing years have dulled the details of her face, but the vivid image of her hands—generous, serving—continues to motivate me as a teacher. She joyfully provided for others, choosing to focus on God's overflowing well of blessings in her life.

In moments of spiritual poverty, I am sometimes overwhelmed with a fear of having nothing to offer in service to those around me. Then the example of that marvelous teacher reminds me that I can afford to be generous because of God's wonderful provision for me. Truly, our Father, "who richly provides us with everything for our enjoyment" has directed us also "to do good, to be rich in good deeds, and to be generous" in our provision for others (1 Timothy 6:17–18).

# THE
# *LOVE*
## of a
# TEACHER

# PEOPLE CHANGE PEOPLE

KEITH J. LEENHOUTS

— from *Father, Son, 3-Mile Run* —

T HE LATE JUDGE Paul Alexander of Toledo, Ohio, a great juvenile court jurist, displayed a sign in his courtroom. It read, "Attitudes are not changed by platitudes. Human conduct is changed by human contact. People change people."

In 1969 at Little Rock, Arkansas, I gained a new appreciation for these words.

Speaking before a group of citizens and professionals about the use of volunteers in court, my attention was drawn to a graying black man who sat in the first row. He seemed to glow—as if there were so much goodness in his soul a flimsy barrier of skin could not contain it. Love radiated from this man and reached out to me. Though he had not said one word all night, his presence dominated the room. One of the most godly-appearing human beings I had ever seen, he fascinated me. I had to get to know him.

After completing my speech, I pressed through the crowd and introduced myself. His name was Luther Black. After a few minutes of polite exchanges, I said, "Mr. Black, I need a ride to the airport tomorrow morning. Could you possibly take me?" Luther said he would, and I asked if he could join me for breakfast, adding, "Luther, I usually like to have a big, leisurely breakfast, so could we meet early?" Truthfully, my normal habit is to gobble a little bread as I run out of the house, late as usual. But I needed to spend time with this man and discover what made him such a remarkable human being. With this ploy I managed to spend almost three hours with Luther Black.

At breakfast the next morning, we chatted for a while about the concept of Volunteers in Probation. Then I asked the question that was really burning in my heart and mind.

"Mr. Black, what makes you the person you are?" I figured that something extraordinary must have happened. Looking at Luther was like looking at the Grand Canyon. Its creation was not the accident of some pioneer stubbing his toe, nor the result of an Indian's kick at the dirt years ago. Rather, incredible forces worked wonders to create one of the world's most grandiose valleys. The same had to be true of Luther. He did not glow with such abundant love without having experienced a defining transformation.

Luther smiled. "Who am I and what am I? Why, what I am goes back to my childhood. Though it was fifty years ago, I remember it like yesterday. I was the youngest of seventeen children on a sharecropper's farm in Arkansas. When I was eight my mother and father made two huge sacrifices so that I might go to school. First, they bought me some good clothes and shoes; and second, they decided they could get along without my help in the fields. I was the first one in the family to ever go to school.

"I remember that first day in school very well. I had never been separated from my brothers and sisters before, and I was terrified. To cover up my fear, I made noise. I tapped the chair in front of me and talked in a loud voice. I was very frightened, and the more frightened I became, the noisier I got.

"Suddenly, a huge figure loomed over me. I raised my head up slow and looked into the face of my teacher. She looked down at me without a smile, but with no meanness in her eyes. In a voice like a person would use for nighttime prayers, she said, 'Little Black, come with me to the front of the room.' She called me 'Little Black' because I was the youngest member of the Black family.

"I dragged my feet, not wanting to follow. I just knew she was going to kick me out of school. What a disappointment I would be to my family. My dad would be very angry and spank me something awful when I got home.

"She interrupted my thoughts and fears as she sat down in her big chair and said, 'Little Black, read to me. Sit on my lap and read to me.'

"Still trembling, I sat on her lap and began to read. And as I read she gave me a hug. The more I read, the more she hugged me. She was a big woman. As I disappeared into her lap and bosom, my fear went away. I have never been afraid since.

"A few weeks later our class held a spelling bee, and I reached the finals. They gave me a word—one of those with an *i* and an *e* in it. I didn't know then, and to this day I still can't remember which comes first. Is it *i* before *e* except after *c*, or *e* before *i* except before *c*—or what? I can't remember the rule.

"I shuffled my feet, stared at the floor, and was about to sit down in defeat when I heard my teacher clear her throat and cough. As I looked up she smiled, winked, and pointed at her eye. I knew the next letter had to be *i*. So I said the letter *i*, spelled the rest of the word, and won the contest. No one ever knew she had helped me. It remained our secret.

"That teacher gave me love when I needed it most. She knew, out of all the students in the classroom, that I needed victory the most. With so much against me, I needed a slight advantage. She bent the rules and helped me. That one victory gave me the boost I needed to achieve in school.

"Sometimes I think that's what love is about—helping someone achieve victory when he can't do it himself. And do it in secret so everyone else thinks he did it on his own.

"You know, she was the most important teacher I ever had, but I hardly remember a word she said. I guess what she taught me was important but not nearly so important as the fact that she loved me and helped me to get something I could not get by myself—victory and self-respect.

"I went on to the University of Arkansas, graduated, and completed post-graduate work at Columbia University. I later became the Director of Public Instruction, Adult Division, for the State of Arkansas. I have received many awards and honors. Plaques and certificates line the walls of my home. But the most important thing that ever happened to me was when my teacher put me on her lap and hugged me."

# PERSISTENT LOVE

CANDY ARRINGTON

S EVERAL YEARS AFTER taking a teaching position at an alternative school, Mrs. Bennett encountered Polly. It quickly became apparent that Polly was her most challenging student yet. Arms folded tightly across a stained, too-small shirt, Polly marched into the classroom, headed for a seat in a far back corner of the room, and flung herself into the chair. Slouching as low as she could go without falling out of the chair, Polly began to casually draw on the desktop. Her greasy, tangled hair slanted across an unwashed face and her hard slash of a mouth mirrored a lifetime of hurts and unmet needs. Mrs. Bennett saw the pain behind the sullen expression and recognized the avoidance of eye contact as a defense mechanism. Polly was definitely going to be a challenge.

Later in the day, Mrs. Bennett called on Polly. "Please sit up in your chair and give us the answer to number seven."

"I dunno." Polly answered without adjusting her position.

Mrs. Bennett let it pass and moved on to another student.

At the end of the day, Mrs. Bennett saw Polly slide by her desk and put something on one corner. After all the students had gone, Mrs. Bennett opened the ill-folded wad of notebook paper and read the smudged words written in cramped, all-but-illegible handwriting: I HATE YOU! The words stabbed her heart as effectively as if she'd experienced a knife wound. Slowly, she took a clean white piece of unlined paper from her bottom drawer and wrote three words across it: I *LOVE* YOU. Mrs. Bennett carefully folded the paper, wrote "Polly" on the outside, and placed it in Polly's desk. She paused to lay her hand on the desk and prayed a silent prayer for wisdom in reaching her troubled student.

That simple act began a pattern. Each day Polly left the I-hate-you note on her teacher's desk and each day Mrs. Bennett responded with an I-love-you note for Polly, coupled with a silent prayer. Sometimes the teacher would include a piece of gum, a quarter, or colorful stickers with her notes. Occasionally, Mrs. Bennett thought she detected an all-but-imperceptible softening in Polly, but always the hope was dashed with the hate note left on her desk at the end of the day.

Mrs. Bennett learned that Polly's early childhood with an alcoholic mother and abusive stepfather led her to a series of foster homes. From these experiences, Polly learned to distrust everything she heard from the mouths of adults.

One day Polly angrily asked, "Why do you love me?"

"Because I care about you and because of God's love," replied Mrs. Bennett.

With that opening, the teacher began adding short Scriptures about God's love in her notes. However, there was never any evidence that these seeds of truth fell on anything other than hard, barren ground.

As the year advanced, Polly seemed to take more interest in school, answering questions correctly in class, completing papers on time, and contributing her artistic talents to group projects. Her teacher made the most of these victories, lavishing Polly with praise and encouragement. But still the notes of hatred continued.

On the last day of school, Polly left with the other students. Disappointment swept over Mrs. Bennett. What had she expected? A hug? A word of thanks? She got neither. Returning to her desk, she was overcome with despair, for there, on the corner, was a Polly note. *Couldn't she get by just this last day without the note of hatred?*

Mrs. Bennett's hand trembled as she reached for the note. This one looked different. Instead of the rumpled notebook paper, she saw a pale pink piece of stationery. Carefully lettered on the outside was "Mrs. Bennett." In the bottom right corner, Polly had drawn a bright purple flower with a chartreuse stem. Mrs. Bennett's heart beat faster as she opened the paper. Inside, written in bold magenta marker, were four simple words that melted her heart—"I LOVE YOU TOO!" Mrs. Bennett smiled as a tiny tear of joy escaped the corner of one eye and slid down her cheek. Her efforts with Polly made a difference after all.

———

Mrs. Bennett's love mirrors God's love for his children. Her love for Polly provides a beautiful illustration of God's persistent pursuit of us even when we are unwilling to acknowledge his love. God meets even a small effort on our part with encouragement and praise. Like this teacher, God continues to say "I love you," despite times when we lash out with anger toward him or run from him. His persistent love waits patiently for our acceptance.

# I Love You More Than Crayons

PEPPER J. STINSON

I T WAS THE FOURTH and last time that I would allow Rachel to borrow classroom supplies, I reminded myself. It seemed every time she needed scissors, crayons, or glue, she had to take a trip to the supply shelf to find the necessary items to finish her assignment. I was trying to instill responsibility into my young students, and Rachel's constant lack of taking care of her own supplies was becoming noticeably apparent. I was willing to share pencils and crayons. Having them handy for my students made things run more smoothly in the classroom. However, in the past few days that hoard seemed to be dwindling. I now felt a little stingy sharing with Rachel, since my stuff always seemed to disappear in the bottomless pit of her desk.

The day before she had asked to borrow scissors. I acknowledged with an affirmative and she, as usual, promised to return them to their proper place. Now she asked for them again.

"Didn't you borrow scissors yesterday?" I asked.

"Yes," she replied.

"Did you remember to return them to the basket?"

Rachel put her head down, refusing to look me in the eye. I asked again.

"Where are the scissors that you used yesterday?"

She shrugged and continued her downward stare.

It was almost recess time. Unwilling to cause a confrontation with Rachel in front of the other students, I sent her to her desk with orders to remain in her seat and we'd discuss this issue while her classmates played outdoors.

Thinking that she might feel somewhat remorseful, I allowed Rachel to sit quietly for a few minutes. Perhaps she would be more willing to tell about the missing scissors when she thought about how she was missing her precious playtime.

"How about looking in your desk and your school box to see if the scissors are there? Perhaps they're way in the back and you just can't find them?" I said. Obediently, she searched through the contents of her desk.

I was becoming annoyed. This wasn't the first time Rachel had tested my patience. She was easily distractible, never completed her work, rarely had her homework agenda signed. Several of the other students complained that she had taken items from their desks. Since I had no proof that Rachel was stealing, I had to believe her. Now that my personal supplies were involved, it became a different matter.

Watching Rachel clean out her desk, I scrutinized her appearance. What a ragamuffin she was. Most of the time she came to school unkempt with her brilliant red hair matted, clothes and body dirty. Her person and personal belongings smelled as if she'd slept with an animal. Every time we had head checks for lice, she was always infested. I wasn't thinking too highly of her parentage at the moment either. Rachel was one of those students who teachers have a hard time getting close to.

I was also thinking of the money I had spent to buy classroom supplies. I was teaching in one of the smallest school districts in the state and money was tight, particularly when it came out of my own family's pocket.

I wanted to know where the scissors were and why she couldn't account for them.

I called Rachel to come up to my desk.

"Rachel, where are all the scissors that you have borrowed?" I asked.

"I don't know. I think at home," she admitted.

Reminding this little girl of my classroom rules was the next step, and I lectured her on the pitfalls of taking things that did not belong to her. I then asked her if she had anything else at home that belonged back at school. She shyly nodded her head yes.

"I have two boxes of crayons, a bunch of pencils, and a bottle of glue," she confessed.

Without asking why she'd taken these things home, I told her to return the items the following day or else she and I would be visiting the principal.

For the first time during the encounter, Rachel shed a tear.

*Good*, I thought. *I got through to her*. I was sure that she would return the missing supplies and we'd have no more incidences.

The soft crying became sniffling and sobbing. I reassured her that if she returned the goods everything would be fine and the matter would be forgotten. However, this child was becoming uncontrollably upset.

"Rachel, it's okay. Mrs. Stinson is not mad at you. I just wanted you to learn that you can't take things that don't belong to you."

"But if I bring the scissors and crayons and glue and pencils back, me and my brother won't have them at home to do our homework and draw pictures with," she wailed.

Suddenly, I wanted to reach out to this child. The teacher-shell that teachers wear when they mean business broke apart and my heart poured out to this little one. I wanted to tell her that she could have anything in the classroom because meeting her needs was far more important than finding my scissors and crayons. In that moment I saw her as a precious little lamb of God. It didn't matter if her hair wasn't shiny and clean; it didn't matter that she smelled of urine or had cat hair all over her clothes. Getting a pair of scissors back was significantly nothing compared to the dignity and worth of a six-year-old.

I attempted to draw her into a great big bear hug. Resistance immediately met my touch. She did not hug back. She stood motionless in my arms. My heart sank. I was used to my hugs being returned by first graders.

I released her and spoke softly. "Rachel, I want you to know that I would have been very happy to let you take some crayons, scissors, and glue home. All you had to do was ask. You may keep the crayons and other things. The next time you need something, please tell me."

I suggested that she get a tissue and wipe her eyes before joining her classmates for the remainder of recess.

As she turned to go, I touched her hand and looked into her beautiful eyes. I couldn't resist saying, "I really do love you."

She quickly and quietly left the room. I was left with an empty room and a very disturbing thought. I had hugged a child and received nothing in return. Had I, as her teacher, been so blind that I missed the signs that Rachel desperately needed love and attention? What was going on in her life, or in her home, that she was unable to demonstrate love? Had life dealt her such a blow that she was unable to respond to a hug? Tearfully, I prayed for Rachel and her family. I also asked forgiveness for my attitude toward this child. I asked for a double dose of love, not only for her, but for other students under my tutelage who needed to know that they are loved. I asked for wisdom that I might demonstrate God's love to all my students, past, present, and future.

The next day, I met Rachel at the door with a smile. I leaned down and whispered in her ear, "Look inside your school box."

She rushed to her desk and pulled out her box. Inside she found her own box of crayons, scissors, glue, and pencils. Questioningly, she looked at me as if to ask, "Are these for me?" I winked and my heart melted when I saw her smile in return.

I prayed for Rachel daily for the next few days. She continued to keep her distance, but was improving in academics and completing her work at school. All was not perfect, but we were making progress.

One afternoon at recess, I surprisingly felt little hands holding on to me. Looking down, it was Rachel. Another student had chased her and evidently she picked me for base. I held her tightly, refusing to let her go. She squealed with delight that I was caught up in the game.

"Mrs. Stinson, let me go, please," she begged.

"I only let go when I get a hug," I insisted.

This time there was no resistance. A child who learned that her teacher loved and accepted her was hugging me. Rachel knew that I loved her more than my crayons.

Eyes brimming with tears, I watched as Rachel and her girl friends ran joyfully back to their play. On a busy, noisy playground I bowed my head and thanked my heavenly Father that he knew that I was a child just like Rachel. There were times in my life when I had needed to be embraced by the Father, but I held back for fear of being rejected and reprimanded. Just like my little redheaded student, I didn't want to bring back the crayons, pencils, and glue of my life and lay them at the feet of the Father. Yet, time and time again, when I gave the goods back to him, he laid them aside, drew me into his arms, and whispered the words to me that I spoke to Rachel that day, "I really do love you."

# LOVE IT BACK TO LIFE, MOTHER

MARGARET JENSEN

⎯ from *First We Have Coffee* ⎯

S TANDING ON THE promises, watching all the girls go by."

The five-year-old singer stood in the reception hall, feet firmly planted and arms folded across his starched white shirt and bow tie. His polished shoes shone on the soft carpet, and his blond hair, parted on one side, was slick and trim. He sang with all the confidence of a seasoned performer and enjoyed the applause of his amused audience—the guests attending the annual open house. This was his first day in the Norwegian Children's Home, Brooklyn, New York.

Mama, unaware of the "one-man show" in the reception hall, was giving her full attention to the last-minute details of hosting the children's home open house.

Enjoying a brief visit to New York, I followed Mama around and was utterly amazed at her ability to attend to innumerable details, when she was continually interrupted to answer a child's question or to make an important decision. She flowed through the days like a river, bringing refreshment to many a dry bank. She reminded me of the man described in Psalm I, who was "a tree planted by the rivers of water."

Mama had received a call. "The board of directors asked me to be the superintendent of the children's home, a place for homeless Norwegian children. The parents of some are very ill. Others are missing or dead. The children from a family are kept together, so here I am, a mother again."

The wise men behind the scenes saw the compassionate heart of a universal mother, and an ability to discipline and motivate others in love. God saw an obedient child, walking out her loving faith in Him who could do anything, who would never fail her.

So, Mama accepted the call to become the superintendent of the Norwegian Children's Home. Papa served as chaplain and social worker. They relinquished the pastorate at the First Norwegian Baptist Church to serve together in the children's home, but the fellowship and worship in their local church continued.

Today was open house. The warm sunlight cast a glow over the neatly trimmed gardens. Every room in the beautiful brick house was in order. The children had been rehearsing songs and readings, and, of course, proper manners. Bright hair bows and matching socks complemented polished shoes, ruffles, and lace. The boys stood like starched penguins, in dark suits and white shirts. Every hair rested in place. Only mischievous eyes refused conformity.

Johnny, the new boy, had arrived in time to be scrubbed, combed, and outfitted in a new suit. He had been told that visitors were coming to see him. He was to stand still and watch. He stood still, but couldn't resist putting on a show.

Within moments of his rendition of standing and watching, he was gathered into perfumed arms and smothered with kisses. When an older boy led him away, Johnny waved happily to all the newfound friends who had come to see him.

Yesterday he had been alone. His mother had been taken to King's County Hospital, and no one could find his father. A distant relative brought him to the "home," where he discovered a new family life.

The ruffled girls swished alongside their guests and excitedly showed them their treasures—quilts they had made for their beds and stuffed animals that kept a silent watch over the neat dormitory. Mama insisted that each child have a box of his or her own in which to store personal treasures. I overheard one girl: "I never had a treasure box before, and no one can peek. I made my quilt. Debbie is five. She is my little sister and I take care of her. I help her dress and lay out her clothes for kindergarten. I braid her pigtails and match her socks and ribbons. I taught her to tie her laces and the bow on her dress. Each one has a brother or sister. Like a family, you know. Some have visitors, but I have no one. Will you be my visitor?"

The older woman, plump and silver-haired, squeezed the girl's hand and, in her soft Norwegian accent, promised to be her visitor. She opened her purse and pulled out a perfumed handkerchief, "Karen, put this in your treasure box, and next time I'll bring you a picture. Perhaps we can take a picture of you, for me to keep." That was the beginning of a long friendship.

"Young man, I understand you'll soon be eighteen and leaving the home."

"Yes, sir, but I don't know where to go," Tom answered the distinguished white-haired executive he was escorting on the tour of the boy's dormitory.

"I'll be your friend and help you get to college, or find a job. Here's my card, just call me anytime. We can always find time to talk things over. By the way, what happened to you, young man? The last time I was here you were skipping out at night and having problems at school. In fact, several of you boys were about to be sent to correctional school. What happened?"

"Mother Tweten, that's what happened.

"I'll never forget the first night she came to our dormitory. We had planned some bold adventures and waited for her to make her rounds. Instead, she sat down on Bob's bed, sang Norwegian songs, and read the Bible and prayed for each one of us by name. She got up and kissed us all good night and told us she loved us. When she left she stood by the door and said, 'God bless you, my boys.' We couldn't carry out our plans. The next night she sat on Ted's bed, told a story, read, sang, and prayed. She kissed us good night and said, 'God bless you, my boys.'

"Then one night she came in and sat on the wrong bed. Bill jumped up and said, 'You sat on Ted's bed twice. It's my turn tonight.' None of us went to reform school. The tough guy, Bill, got saved at the Billy Graham Crusade in Madison Square Garden. The next night he made Bob go forward. 'Get saved or I'll beat you up!' he said."

Downstairs in the dining room an air of festivity reigned. The older boys cared for the younger, and the guests were served by happy children. Church groups and women's clubs mingled with dignitaries from government, businessmen, and news reporters. The children sensed their importance and rose with honor to the occasion. This was a special day; Mama had made them a part of the festivities.

No one had believed that 40 to 50 children could be beautifully disciplined in gracious courtesy. But they didn't know Mama! Papa, handsome as ever, enjoyed the guests and with great flourish practiced all his old Norwegian jokes. The businessmen who had founded the home looked at their fulfilled dream. Mama saw the thread of love that had been interwoven between frightened children and these adults—lonely immigrants who had persevered at building schools, hospitals, even the children's home. Mama was proud of her children. When they performed before their enthusiastic audience, a sense of worth crept into their once frightened, empty hearts. They basked in the love and approval of their mother and felt safe within the walls of their home.

To conclude the day's program, Mama told the story of the dead plant.

"One day Susie came in from the playground, holding a broken pot with a wilted plant in her muddy hands.

"She begged me, 'Please don't throw away the plant.'

" 'But Susie, the plant is dead,' I said.

" 'Then you must love it back to life, Mother.'

"She thrust the wilted plant into my hand and skipped away, completely confident that its life would return. I placed the remains of this plant in a new flowerpot filled with fresh dirt. The sun filtered through the Brooklyn skies and warmed the lifeless plant that sat on my windowsill. Every day I watered my little wilted garden and waited. One day a green shoot appeared, and now a lovely green plant thrives on my sill.

"When someone brings us a frightened, wilted, hurt child, I hear my Susie say, 'Love it back to life, Mother!' So many human relationships can be loved back to life. For me the most rewarding are those with a child, who has been wilted and abandoned in a broken flowerpot or home. For a child who then is thrust into my hand, 'Love him back to life' is my highest command. You people of Norway gave me a flowerpot, this lovely home, and God pours His love through us—to love them back to life.

"I thank you."

The sun set over the gardens and brick walls. The children were tucked in their beds. The steps of the guests had echoed down the walk. The door had closed behind them. Mama sat down to a quiet cup of coffee. The amber glow of love had wrapped a warm blanket over the weak and strong together. She opened her Bible and read, "Inasmuch as ye have done it unto one of the least of these my brethren, ye have done it unto me" (Matthew 25:40).

# THE
# *INSPIRATION*
# *of a*
# TEACHER

# REVENGE OF THE HIGH-SCHOOL MATH TEACHER

CARON LOVELESS

from *The Words That Inspired the Dreams*

*The dreams begin with a teacher who believes in you,*
*who tugs and pushes and leads you on to the next plateau,*
*sometimes poking you with a sharp stick called truth.*
(DAN RATHER)

K EVIN WAS EVERY teacher's worst nightmare. He had a knack for clowning around that went beyond the normal, expected antics of most high-school boys. When he walked into class at the start of a new term, everyone grinned and nudged each other. They knew from experience that if Kevin's name was on the roll, their class would be a riot.

It seemed that Kevin's main goal in life was to get attention. And at an early age, he had discovered that the best way to get attention was to do something outrageous.

One night, as the eight-year-old mascot at a high-school basketball game, Kevin spotted the opposing team's mascot dressed up in a tiger suit. Suddenly the idea came to him to yank off the tiger's tail. In a flash, he scampered across the gym and made his heist. That stunt won him banner headlines in the next school newspaper and fueled his jets for even more tricks.

In high school, Kevin was known for crawling out of class on his hands and knees and setting trash cans on fire. Once he even talked the whole school into putting alarm clocks in their lockers and setting them to go off at 2:00 P.M.

Scholarship was not Kevin's forte. In his senior year, he gave his math teacher such a hard time that she resigned from teaching. With graduation just months away, Kevin, who had been failing math, was assigned to another teacher who tutored him after school in her own home. Her name was Eleanor Wilson, and she was neither distressed nor impressed with Kevin's rowdy reputation.

One day when Mrs. Wilson saw Kevin in the hall, she pulled him aside, looked him straight in the eye, and asked, "Kevin, when are you going to stop playing your game?"

"What game is that, Teach?"

"The game that you play best," she smiled. "Being the worst!"

At the time, Kevin laughed and tried to slough off the comment. But somehow her words rang true, and at odd times for the rest of his life, he would still hear her speaking them.

Soon after this encounter, Kevin sought to channel the abundance of his negative energy in a more positive direction. He went in to see the school guidance counselor and said, "I've been doing some heavy thinking, and I want to go to college." But the counselor just looked up through his glasses and remarked, "With your record, I couldn't get you admitted to reform school."

Kevin had lost valuable time and was ill-prepared for higher education. By his last semester, he ranked fourth from the bottom of his class. But he was determined to get into college. He applied to 160 schools and was turned down by every one of them. Finally, after receiving letters from his older brother and his pastor, North Park College in Chicago agreed to enroll him—but only on probation.

Kevin didn't last long at North Park. By his second year, he was failing classes and reverting to pranks. And when he and a roommate were caught raiding the conscience fund of the college ice-cream machine, the dean firmly showed him the exit.

With this setback, Kevin was forced to move out west with his parents and enter the world of work, which he had been desperately hoping to avoid. He had no skills or training, so he got a job as a janitor, making $195 a month. It wasn't long before Kevin figured out that the janitor job was going nowhere. Convinced he was made for better things, Kevin tried college again, this time enrolling in a night course at the University of Arizona. But he flunked that too.

Then one day while he was emptying a trash can, Kevin spied an attractive girl coming down the hall. She was a nurse's aide in the building where he worked. He brashly waltzed up to her and asked, "How would you like to go to the New York World's Fair with me?" The girl turned him down for the fair but agreed to lunch at McDonald's. It was this girl, Sande (who later became his wife), who encouraged Kevin to explore a relationship with Jesus Christ. And when he did, the downward spiral of his life took a definite turn upward.

Kevin went back to the University of Arizona and took another course. This time, he made the highest grade in a class of six hundred. After that, he went on to get his undergraduate, master's, and doctoral degrees, managing to stay on the dean's list for most of that time.

During those years, Kevin often thought of Mrs. Wilson and her belief in him. Her corrective encouragement—plus a comment made by Sande's supervisor, who said, "Don't associate with that janitor; he'll never amount to anything"[1]—kept him motivated toward success.

Today, the kid who was either emptying trash cans or setting them on

---

[1]Kevin Leman, *The Birth Order Book* (Old Tappen, N.J.; Fleming H. Revell Company, 1985).

fire is now internationally known Christian psychologist and conference speaker Dr. Kevin Leman. He is the consulting psychologist for *Good Morning America* and has authored more than seventeen books, including *The New Birth Order Book, Sex Begins in the Kitchen,* and *Becoming a Couple of Promise.*

Amazingly, God used the stern but loving words of a wise teacher to turn a disorderly young schoolboy into a dedicated Christian leader who would one day write a best-selling book called *Making Your Children Mind without Losing Yours.*

## YOU MIGHT LIKE TO KNOW

Dr. Kevin Leman held the post of assistant dean of students at the University of Arizona for eleven years. He has been a guest on *Oprah, Larry King Live, CBS Good Morning,* and *The Today Show* as well as the *Focus on the Family* radio program with Dr. James Dobson. Dr. Leman also hosts a radio program, *Parent Talk,* with Randy Carlson.

Several years ago, Dr. Leman visited his former math teacher, Mrs. Wilson, to thank her for the challenge she gave him in those closing weeks of high school. She smiled and humbly said, "Oh, I did very little, Kevin. You did it yourself. You were a challenge, all right, but I knew you could do it if you wanted to!"

Other words that highly impacted Dr. Leman came in 1981 from fellow psychologist and author James Dobson. The two were having lunch in Arcadia, California, and Dr. Leman asked Dr. Dobson to give him one good piece of advice for his life. Dobson thought a minute then said, "Just run everything by [your wife] first."

# THE STRANGER WHO TAUGHT MAGIC

ARTHUR GORDON

—— from *A Touch of Wonder* ——

THAT JULY MORNING, I remember, was like any other, calm and opalescent before the heat of the fierce Georgia sun. I was 13, sunburned, shaggy-haired, a little aloof, and solitary. In winter I had to put on shoes and go to school like everyone else. But summers I lived by the sea, and my mind was empty and wild and free.

On this particular morning, I had tied my rowboat to the pilings of an old dock upriver from our village. There, sometimes, the striped sheepshead lurked in the still, green water. I was crouched, motionless as a stone, when a voice spoke suddenly above my head: "Canst thou draw out leviathan with a hook? or his tongue with a cord which thou lettest down?"

I looked up, startled, into a lean pale face and a pair of the most remarkable eyes I had ever seen. It wasn't a question of color; I'm not sure, now, what color they were. It was a combination of things: warmth, humor, interest, alertness. *Intensity*—that's the word, I guess—and, underlying it all, a curious kind of mocking sadness. I believe I thought him old.

He saw how taken aback I was. "Sorry," he said. "It's a bit early in the morning for the Book of Job, isn't it?" He nodded at the two or three fish in the boat. "Think you could teach me how to catch those?"

Ordinarily, I was wary of strangers, but anyone interested in fishing was hardly a stranger. I nodded, and he climbed down into the boat. "Perhaps we should introduce ourselves," he said. "But then again, perhaps not. You're a boy willing to teach, I'm a teacher willing to learn. That's introduction enough. I'll call you *Boy,* and you call me *Sir.*"

Such talk sounded strange in my world of sun and salt water. But there was something so magnetic about the man, and so disarming about his smile; that I didn't care.

I gave him a hand line and showed him how to bait his hooks with fiddler crabs. He kept losing baits, because he could not recognize a sheepshead's stealthy tug, but he seemed content not to catch anything. He told me he had rented one of the weathered bungalows behind the dock. "I needed to hide for a while," he said. "Not from the police, or anything like that. Just from friends and relatives. So don't tell anyone you've found me, will you?"

I was tempted to ask where he was from; there was a crispness in the way he spoke that was very different from the soft accents I was accustomed to. But I didn't. He had said he was a teacher, though, and so I asked what he taught.

"In the school catalog they call it English," he said. "But I like to think of it as a course in magic—in the mystery and magic of words. Are you fond of words?"

I said that I had never thought much about them. I also pointed out that the tide was ebbing, that the current was too strong for more fishing, and that in any case it was time for breakfast.

"Of course," he said, pulling in his line. "I'm a little forgetful about such things these days." He eased himself back onto the dock with a little grimace, as if the effort cost him something. "Will you be back on the river later?"

I said that I would probably go casting for shrimp at low tide.

"Stop by," he said. "We'll talk about words for a while, and then perhaps you can show me how to catch shrimp."

So began a most unlikely friendship, because I did go back. To this day, I'm not sure why. Perhaps it was because, for the first time, I had met an adult on terms that were in balance. In the realm of words and ideas, he might be the teacher. But in my own small universe of winds and tides and sea creatures, the wisdom belonged to me.

Almost every day after that, we'd go wherever the sea gods or my whim decreed. Sometimes up the silver creeks, where the terrapin skittered down the banks and the great blue herons stood like statues. Sometimes along the ocean dunes, fringed with graceful sea oats, where by night the great sea turtles crawled and by day the wild goats browsed. I showed him where the mullet swirled and where the flounder lay in cunning camouflage. I learned that he was incapable of much exertion; even pulling up the anchor seemed to exhaust him. But he never complained. And, all the time, talk flowed from him like a river.

Much of it I have forgotten now, but some comes back as clear and distinct as if it all happened yesterday, not decades ago. We might be sitting in a hollow of the dunes, watching the sun go down in a smear of crimson. "Words," he'd say. "Just little black marks on paper. Just sounds in the empty air. But think of the power they have! They can make you laugh or cry, love or hate, fight or run away. They can heal or hurt. They even come to look and sound like what they mean. Angry looks angry on the page. Ugly sounds ugly when you say it. Here!" He would hand me a piece of shell. "Write a word that looks or sounds like what it means."

I would stare helplessly at the sand.

"Oh," he'd cry, "you're being dense. There are so many! Like *whisper* . . . *leaden* . . . *twilight* . . . *chime*. Tell you what: When you go to bed tonight, think of five words that look like what they mean and five that sound like what they mean. Don't go to sleep until you do!"

And I would try—but always fall asleep.

Or we might be anchored just offshore, casting into the surf for sea bass, our little bateau nosing over the rollers like a restless hound.

"Rhythm," he would say. "Life is full of it; words should have it, too. But you have to train your ear. Listen to the waves on a quiet night; you'll pick up the cadence. Look at the patterns the wind makes in dry sand and you'll see how syllables in a sentence should fall. Do you know what I mean?"

My conscious self didn't know; but perhaps something deep inside me did. In any case, I listened.

I listened, too, when he read from the books he sometimes brought: Kipling, Conan Doyle, Tennyson's *Idylls of the King*. Often he would stop and repeat a phrase or a line that pleased him. One day, in Malory's *Le Morte d'Arthur*, he found one: "And the great horse grimly neighed." "Close your eyes," he said to me, "and say that slowly, out loud." I did. "How did it make you feel?" "It gives me the shivers," I said truthfully. He was delighted.

But the magic that he taught was not confined to words; he had a way of generating in me an excitement about things I had always taken for granted. He might point to a bank of clouds. "What do you see there? Colors? That's not enough. Look for towers and drawbridges. Look for dragons and griffins and strange and wonderful beasts."

Or he might pick up an angry claw-brandishing blue crab, holding it cautiously by the back flippers as I had taught him. "Pretend you're this crab," he'd say. "What do you see through those stalklike eyes? What do you feel with those complicated legs? What goes on in your tiny brain? Try it for just five seconds. Stop being a boy. Be a crab!" And I would stare in amazement at the furious creature, feeling my comfortable identity lurch and sway under the impact of the idea. So the days went by. Our excursions became less frequent, because he tired so easily. He brought two chairs down to the dock and some books, but he didn't read much. He seemed content to watch me as I fished, or the circling gulls, or the slow river coiling past.

A sudden shadow fell across my life when my parents told me I was going to camp for two weeks. On the dock that afternoon I asked my friend if he would be there when I got back. "I hope so," he said gently.

But he wasn't. I remember standing on the sun-warmed planking of the old dock, staring at the shuttered bungalow and feeling a hollow sense of finality and loss. I ran to Jackson's grocery store—where everyone knew everything—and asked where the schoolteacher had gone.

"He was sick, real sick," Mrs. Jackson replied. "Doc phoned his relatives up north to come get him. He left something for you—he figured you'd be asking for him."

She handed me a book. It was a slender volume of verse, *Flame and Shadow,* by someone I had never heard of: Sara Teasdale. The corner of one page was turned down, and there was a penciled star by one of the poems. I still have the book, with the poem "On the Dunes."

If there is any life when death is over,
These tawny beaches will know much of me,
I shall come back, as constant and as changeful
As the unchanging, many-colored sea.
If life was small, if it has made me scornful;
Forgive me; I shall straighten like a flame
In the great calm of death, and if you want me,
Stand on the sea-ward dunes and call my name.

Well, I have never stood on the dunes and called his name. For one thing, I never knew it; for another, I'd be too self-conscious. And there are long stretches when I forget all about him. But sometimes—when the music or the magic in a phrase makes my skin tingle, or when I pick up an angry blue crab, or when I see a dragon in the flaming sky—sometimes I remember.

# GRACE NOTES

JEANNE ZORNES

THE MOMENT I dreaded had come. I felt the sweat oozing onto my forehead and pouring out of my armpits as I wobbled on nervous legs to the junior high practice room. There, in front of orchestra teacher Mr. McNamara, I would have my first playing test. It was 1959 and I was a seventh grader sitting in the last chair of the junior high orchestra. The other kids in the orchestra had played their instruments since fifth grade, but three of us in the back row were beginners, there by special permission.

"She'll catch on fast," Mr. McNamara assured my parents after learning I'd taken a few years of piano lessons and could read music. He taught all the district's string students, grade school through high school. I was awed by him and his ability to play not just string bass—his main instrument—but also violin, viola, and cello.

I'd gotten frustrated in piano because my fingers were too short to reach a full octave. Violin offered me hope of becoming a real musician. Besides, we already had an instrument—one my dad played as a twelve-year-old in 1928.

Dad's music career had lasted one year. He sang even worse than he played. Even as an adult in church, his guesses at hymn melodies only made people stare or giggle. Mom could pick out melodies on the piano with her right hand, but she couldn't do left-hand chords. With neither parent a musician, I was on my own except for the teaching of Mr. McNamara.

At first, I found tuning the strings and playing simple songs exciting. I looked forward to each class with this tall, thin man with a crew cut and dark-framed glasses. Behind thick lenses were eyes that focused just on each student as if to say, "I care and want you to love orchestra." Soon, however, I became discouraged by the physical discomfort of the instrument. My fingers stung, my chin hurt, and my shoulders ached. Despite my best efforts, I played poorly. I wondered if I'd ever improve to the level of the other kids in the junior high orchestra.

So when the day of the playing test came, I considered staying home sick. Yet I knew that delaying it wouldn't solve my problems. Instead, I showed up in my favorite pleated blue skirt and matching blouse. I hoped looking nice would help me forget I was a skinny, pimply kid with impossible hair who squawked out-of-tune notes. My sense of impending failure rose with each step I took down the platform to the testing room, past the first-chair concertmistress whose skills intimidated me.

As I came into the room, Mr. McNamara looked weary as he opened a music book to an easy number. My knees shook with fear. I wiped my sweaty hands on my skirt.

"Let's try this one," he said, showing me a piece I'd practiced many times.

I couldn't play more than a few measures before my fingers and bow got out of sync.

"Let's try again."

I did, with worse results. I pulled the violin away from my chin with such frustration that it slipped out of my hands and fell on the floor with a dull clunk. I felt my heart race as I thought the worst—that I'd broken it. What would my dad say?

I cried.

Mr. McNamara picked up my violin like a precious baby. He shook it gently to make sure the sound post hadn't popped out of place, checked its corners, then re-tuned the strings.

"It seems okay," he said. "Let's try again."

I stared at the floor, tightening my face muscles in a useless attempt to keep more tears from spilling. I'd never catch up. I glanced up at Mr. McNamara, expecting him to chide me for my mistakes.

Instead, he looked at me kindly and said, "I want you to know you're making good progress. Just keep practicing. You'll make it."

He let me wipe my tears before I returned, head down but heart lifted, to the orchestra room. Just those few words had rekindled my passion to practice, even when my fingers throbbed and my neck ached. I practiced at school, in my bedroom, and in the bathroom where the tile walls made the sound a little richer and I could watch my bowing in the mirror.

I later thought how much alike God and Mr. McNamara worked in my life. When I was young in my faith, comparing myself to those older and seasoned in spiritual things, I felt like a failure. But when I cried out in frustration to God, he responded in kindness and understanding. I still needed to practice spiritual disciplines, like prayer and Bible study. But he delighted in encouraging me because he knew each little effort, each time I corrected a sour attitude, brought me closer to his great plan for my life.

By the way, Mr. McNamara was still the orchestra teacher when I reached my senior year of high school, the fruit of his encouragement. That year, I sat in the honored first-chair spot of concertmistress.

# THE TICKET

PATRICIA S. LAYE

FOR THIRTY-ONE YEARS I worked as a school social worker, my primary job being to find and bring in truant children. The difficult part was to discover why they refused to attend school and how to correct this situation. One year a fourteen-year-old boy's name repeatedly appeared on my referral sheet. A ninth grader, he was polite, yet angry at the world. His teachers told me that he was gifted but showed little interest in his schoolwork and less in attending classes.

I picked him up as I had many times before, and as we drove to school I asked him why he continued to play hooky when he knew I'd find him.

"Why should I go to school? My daddy's a drunk who's always gone playing in his blues band. My mother works at a bar all the time, so I never see her. No matter how hard she works, we never have enough money. I don't have anything. I'm poor and I'll always be poor."

Such resignation in his voice made my heart ache for him. We were headed to the high school, but I turned in the opposite direction toward downtown.

Surprised, he looked over at me and said, "Hey, where are you taking me?"

"I want to show you something."

We drove to an area of town called The Push, where the streets were lined with winos, drug addicts, pimps, prostitutes, all with the same hopeless expressions on their faces as his.

I slowed the car and pointed. "Take a good look at these people. Your teachers tell me that you're very bright. Some of these people may even be smarter than you, but they gave up. Now you have a choice. You can whine, feel sorry for yourself, wind up here, and remain bogged down in poverty, or you can use the wonderful mind you have. You can avoid The Push."

"How?" He looked at me as if I were crazy.

"Your mind is a gift from God. He's given you a one-way ticket out of poverty. The decision to escape is up to you. Neither I nor anyone else can use that ticket for you."

He pointed to his soiled shirt. "Look at my clothes. They're always dirty. I don't have any clean clothes. My mother's too tired or hung over to wash. I'm ashamed to go to school stinking. The kids laugh and make fun of me."

"Will you meet me after school?"

"Sure."

"I'm going to teach you something today."

I didn't know if I'd see him again, but that afternoon he was waiting when I pulled up at the high school. We drove to his home. I saw his reluctance to let me go inside. "It's all right," I assured him. "I'm here to help you."

The house turned out to be as filthy as I'd expected, with garbage cans running over, unwashed dishes on the table, beds unmade, and a huge pile of beer cans and liquor bottles beside a recliner in their living room. I knew how depressing it must be to live in such a home.

"I'm sorry things are such a mess," he said, walking to a filthy worn couch and shoving the dirty clothes, potato chip bags, and soft drink cans onto the floor. "You want to sit down?"

I smiled and my heart ached at his attempt to be hospitable. "No, we need to get busy. Will you show me where your washing machine is?"

He took me to a back porch where clothes lay piled in a mound on the floor. Here again were sacks of rotting garbage and trash. I wondered if I could stand the smell without gagging. "I have a suggestion," I said. "While I fill the washing machine, why don't you gather up all your dirty clothes? After that why don't you pick up all the garbage and haul it to the curb? I have a box of garbage bags in that shopping bag I brought with me."

I showed him how to sort clothes and we chatted until the machine was loaded. Then rolling up my sleeves, I said, "Now, let's tackle this house. If you'll pick up the trash on the floors, I'll take this broom and sweep."

I wondered what his mother would say if she came home early and saw us cleaning her house. Somehow I thought she'd be embarrassed, but I didn't think the shame would carry over to any improvement in housekeeping. My only hope was to teach this young man to take pride in a clean home.

After a couple of hours, the laundry was done and we had become friends. As we surveyed the results of our hard work, I suggested that he help his mother by occasionally straightening up the house. I said, "She'll be surprised to come home to a clean house. It's a way to show that you appreciate the long hours she works to feed and clothe you." The grin on his face told me how proud he was of his efforts.

I pulled out three new changes of clothes from the shopping bag and handed them to him. "See if these fit you."

"I can't pay for them. I don't have any money." He glanced longingly at the clothes before handing them back.

"These are a gift from a local church and a merchant who have faith in you and want to see you succeed. They enjoy secretly helping young people."

"How can I thank them if I don't know who they are?"

"By making good grades again and attending school every day. Is this a deal?" I held up my hand for a high five.

He laughed and hit his hand against mine. "It's a deal."

Every six weeks I checked on the boy. I dropped by his house and each time it would be clean, with a place for me to sit. He soon started fixing us a soft drink and serving it while I looked at his report card bragging on his excellent grades. I was so pleased with his attitude and change in behavior that I promised him I'd do my best to see that he got a scholarship to college when he graduated.

When he turned sixteen, a merchant gave him an afternoon job. He began paying for his own clothes, taking the rest home to help his mother. I continued to follow his progress as he soared to the top of all his classes. We spoke often when we met in the halls. I always asked about his family and how things were with him.

One day early in the fall of his senior year he came by my office with a distraught expression on his face. He said, "My daddy died, so Mama and I are moving away to be closer to my grandparents."

I was sorry to hear this, but I tried to conceal my disappointment and fears that he might not succeed elsewhere. Instead I wished him well and told him to contact me when he enrolled in his new school. I reminded him to apply for a college scholarship and assured him I'd help, if he needed me. "Now promise me you'll never give up. Please don't forget the ticket you hold." I never heard from him again, but I always wondered how he turned out.

A few years ago my eighty-year-old aunt needed cataract surgery, so I flew to the state where she lived to be with her. When we arrived at the hospital for the outpatient surgery, the nurse told me that the doctor wished to speak with me before the operation. I worried that perhaps there was some complication as I followed the nurse back to the doctor's office.

While I waited I fretted over what might be wrong with my aunt, dwelling on the worst possible scenario. When the doctor entered the room, he grinned. "Do you remember me?"

At first I couldn't place his face or the name, so many children had passed through my life. Then he reminded me that he was the young boy I'd helped. He said, "When we moved away, I didn't know if I'd make it or not. But I kept remembering that ticket you told me I held. I signed up for ROTC at the new high school and entered college on that scholarship. After graduation from medical college, I served in the Army to repay the obligation. Now I'm in private practice." The same pride he'd exhibited when showing me his report card glowed on his face. "I always wanted to thank you for what you did for me. You were the first person who ever showed any faith in me or acted like I had a chance to pull myself out of the poverty.

"When I read your aunt's records and saw you listed as next of kin, I asked if you were the same person I remembered. I've waited a long time to say thank you, but I'm saying it today."

My heart filled with such joy that I struggled not to embarrass him by tearing up. We talked for a while and then my aunt had her surgery. Later, when I returned to the hospital to clear up my aunt's bill, the nurse handed me a receipt and smiled. The doctor's portion of the bill read, "N/C— paid in advance with a ticket out of poverty."

Although I wasn't a classroom teacher, God worked through me to help others. Seeing the scared young boy eventually reach his potential made all the years of struggling to keep children in school reward enough for my efforts.

# THE
# *WISDOM*
## *of a*
# TEACHER

# WHAT FOLLOWING LOOKS LIKE

### GORDON MACDONALD

—— from *Mid-Course Correction* ——

I HAVE HAD THE PRIVILEGE of knowing many men and women of extraordinary character in the years of my life. But one man stands out among them all. His name was Marvin Goldberg. I write "was" because he died not long ago.

I met Marvin Goldberg when I left my Colorado home to attend the Stony Brook School on Long Island, New York. Soon after I arrived, he went to work on my hidden life.

I was fifteen years old. My recollection was that I was small, physically puny, socially immature, and academically mediocre. My fantasy was to be a prep school football player, a star running back. But the dream was not so mercifully put to death during the first week of fall practice. It became abundantly clear that I lacked the required nerve as well as the pounds to carry a football up the middle and into the line. I was fast, however.

My first conversation with Goldberg was in conjunction with the Stony Brook track-and-field program, which he directed as head coach.

"I'd like you to come down to the field tomorrow and work out with a few of the track men," he said. "I think we might make a runner out of you."

The next day I appeared in shorts and sneakers and ran a few wind sprints for him. He made a few encouraging comments about my running style and suggested I come back again the next day. I did, and I kept coming each day after that. There was something about Marvin Goldberg that made you want to be near him. You knew instantly that he would bring the best out of you, that he would care for you in ways that far exceeded the world of the quarter-mile oval. Something deep within said, "Stick with this man, and you're going to grow." Even as a fifteen-year-old I was perceptive enough to get that message.

In a few weeks, Coach Goldberg had me working out as a potential member of the relay team that would compete at the annual Penn Relays in Philadelphia. He spent hours teaching me how to burst out of the starting blocks, how to bring my body up slowly from the starting crouch to full running position. I learned how to pump my arms, to lengthen my stride, to relax the muscles of my neck and face so that I would not cut off my wind. Members of the team were taught how to hand off the relay baton in full stride inside the "box" in accordance with the rules of relay racing. Goldberg was a perfectionist about these things and showed us movies of teams that had lost close races because a hand off was muffed or because stride was broken.

Each day there would be carefully designed and individualized workouts to strengthen the body and bring stamina to the heart and lungs. The Englishman Roger Bannister had just broken the four-minute-mile barrier and had presented the runner's world an entirely new understanding of athletic conditioning. The fact was, Bannister demonstrated, the athlete had a much greater capacity for development than anyone had ever thought. Coach Goldberg agreed with that assessment, and he proceeded to push us harder than any Stony Brook athletes had been pushed before. "The practices during the week will be painful at times," he told us, "but you'll come to learn that the race on Saturday will be a pleasure."

Although I came to the track team as something of a sprinter, Coach Goldberg soon had me running on his cross-country team (five miles). "It will build your endurance," he said, "and it will be good for the battle you face in your mind." The coach knew that, in the end, a large part of competition on the track is psychological.

Each afternoon we came to the track and checked a bulletin board that displayed each runner's workout plan for the day. Most of us dreaded this moment as we read the coach's latest menu for "suffering." As we read the schedule written in his distinct handwriting, we would silently protest, "There's no way I can do this." And then we would go out and do it for him! He was tough, but we trusted that if he said we could do it, we would be able to do it.

Coach Goldberg was not only committed to developing runners. He made no secret of the fact that he had a passion for building men (Stony Brook was at that time a boys' school). Every bit of an athletic experience, as far as the coach was concerned, was tied tightly to some aspect of character development. He believed in the hidden life and in its deliberate cultivation. And he made it happen in the context of our athletic world.

In my first competitive experience, I was entered in the 200-meter. There were six runners including me on the starting line, but it was clear that my most serious challenge would come from a runner named Alverez who wore the uniform of the Trinity Pawling School. He was big, seemed a bit overweight, walked about heavily. As I pounded the spikes that would hold my starting blocks in place, I actually dared to say to Coach Goldberg, "I don't think I'll have any trouble taking him."

Soon we were crouched in our blocks. The starter barked the traditional commands ("Runners, on your marks . . ."), and the gun sounded. All six runners shot up and out of their starting positions and down the straightaway. About twenty-two seconds later Alverez won going away.

As I walked dejectedly back along the track, Coach Goldberg joined me. "Gordie [I was Gordie in those days and remain that today only to my wife], I have something to say to you. When you told me that you would have no trouble beating Alverez, I knew you had lost the race already. And I decided to let you lose it even though it might hurt the overall team scoring.

"Gordie, you must never, ever underestimate a competitor on the basis of what he looks like or what you've heard about him. First of all, you judged him on the basis of his body and not on the basis of his heart. Until you know what's in a man, you'll never know what the man is.

"Second, you must *never* measure yourself against a competitor; you measure only against yourself. And this is the way it will be all the way through life. If your eyes are on what you think your competitors are going to do and not on the best you yourself can do, you'll lose all kinds of races over and over again."

I never underestimated a competitor on the track ever again. And as hard as it was, I learned from moments like these in the company of Marvin Goldberg never to match myself—intellectually, professionally, spiritually—against anyone else in my adult life. The coach was laying the tracks for the day when it would become clear to me as a biblical person that all of life is played for an audience of One and never as a competition against my peers.

Many races later, I found myself one day at the starting line of the 400 meters. Once again the coach was there with me. The name of the runner to beat was Carlin. "Now, Gordie, I'd like you to come off the blocks in total relaxation. Get up on Carlin's shoulder and stay there. Stay there! Don't try going around him until you're coming off the last turn. Then kick with all you've got. Carlin has superior speed, but you have conditioning. Your race—and I want this to be your race—is in your kick, and you can do your best if you'll trust in the stamina you've built up. You'll have *more* in the last forty yards because we've trained you to have more. So wait until the end and kick! You don't want to get into a serious sprint with Carlin or anyone else in the first three-fourths of the race. Wait for the last turn, remember! Now go do your best."

The race began, and as I'd been told, I came up to Carlin's shoulder.

But as I rounded the *first* turn, I made a decision to depart from the plan. Carlin didn't seem to be running as fast as I'd anticipated. It would be nice, I thought, to lead this race all the way. I remember thinking about the girlfriend at trackside who had come to see me compete. She would be impressed, I thought. Thus, to get her attention as much as anything, I blew past Carlin as we moved up the backstretch.

It was a serious mistake. No sooner had I cleared him than he exploded and passed me as if I were standing still. I never caught Carlin, and he won by ten yards.

"Gordie, I think we need to think about what happened here," Coach Goldberg was saying minutes later. "Did you not hear my instructions, or did you simply choose to ignore them when you started running?"

"Sir, I'm afraid I chose to do things my own way." The tradition of Stony Brookers was to address their seniors as "sir" or "ma'am."

"I'm not half as concerned about the fact that a race was lost as I am about the habit pattern I see in you. You do not listen well. And this problem is going to mark your entire life. It is beginning to look to me as if you will have to learn all the important lessons of life the hard way instead of learning from those who can point the way for you. I wonder how many more races you'll have to lose before you master these things? And I wonder how many mistakes you'll make in life until you figure this out?"

The coach's rebuke was more painful than his workouts. I had let him down terribly. How long, I wondered, would he put up with a foolish athlete who took up a lot of his valuable time all week in practice and then failed him in the race? I left the track that day vowing that I would stop learning lessons, if possible, the hard way. I have worked at this ever since. Marvin Goldberg was the first person to make me aware of this serious flaw in my hidden life in a way that I could see it clearly.

In another of my books I recounted the day when I ran the first leg for our mile relay team at the Penn Relays. Our team had been assigned the second lane. Starting in the first lane was the team from Poly Prep in

Brooklyn. Their leadoff runner was a well-known sprinter who held a conference record for the 100-yard dash.

I have told the story elsewhere of his greeting when we shook hands prior to getting into our starting blocks. "May the best man win," he said. "I'll be waiting for you at the finish line."

Batons in hand, the eight runners took off at the sound of the starter's gun. Within twenty-five yards the runner from Poly Prep had disappeared around the first turn. In my mind I began to settle early for second place on my leg of the relay. And then, about three hundred yards into the race, I saw the runner from Poly Prep just ahead, barely jogging. The seven of us flashed past him as if he were standing still. I like to finish the story with a grin and slyly say, "In kindness I waited for the man from Poly Prep at the finish line."

But that is not the end of the story. Coach Goldberg was also at the finish line. He wanted to talk as soon as the race was over. And when the fourth runner on our team had crossed the line some three minutes later, the two of us, coach and athlete, walked the infield grass together. All about were dozens of other runners warming up for their races, and surrounding us in the stadium were forty thousand noisy spectators. Marvin Goldberg was oblivious to all of them.

"Gordie, I heard what he said to you before the race started. And I want you to remember all your life what happened. The man could easily have beaten you or anyone else if the race had been only 220 yards. But the race was 440 yards long, and he wasn't prepared for that distance. You were. He had speed, but you had stamina.

"And that's going to be the lesson of life. Learn the difference between speed and stamina, and don't confuse the two. What good is a man who can run fast but can't finish the race? Always run to finish, Gordie, always run to finish ... and to finish strong." As he said this, the coach put his hand on my shoulder and looked me straight in the eye. Looking back, I believe he sensed the greatest challenge I would have in my architecture of character. And he was using the story of a race to build what he hoped would be a better man.

# THE KEY TO ESCAPE

LEE EZELL

from *The Cinderella Syndrome*

KATHY ARRIVED AT OUR Bible study a little late. She quickly sat down in the back row and focused her attention on what was being said. I couldn't help but notice the sweet expressions that fleeted across her young face from time to time.

A few months before, she had started coming to our women's group. And she was a far different woman today from the one she had been when we first got to know her. At that time anger had often flashed in her clear blue eyes, and beneath them dark circles spoke of her deep inner exhaustion.

After several brief conversations, I had learned that Kathy was the weary mother of two children with special challenges: one severely retarded and one with a puzzling, chronic reading disability. She was a Christian, yes. Some longing for help had kept her coming to these strengthening times of fellowship. But she was seething in her spirit. As far as she was concerned, God had given her more than her portion of pain.

Not one of us could disagree. "Why?" Kathy asked me one day, fighting back tears. "I asked Him to let my second baby be okay. I begged Him. And I believed. I really did. So why?"

What could I say to her? Any problems I had ever faced vanished when contrasted with the ceaseless struggle Kathy lived with.

"I don't have an answer to that question, Kathy. Nobody on this earth does. All I can tell you is that, barring a miracle, your circumstances aren't going to change. Somehow, someway, you've got to find a means of being peaceful within those terrible circumstances."

"Oh, really? Well, you try it!" she had snapped at me and turned away. Over the course of some weeks our group had been searching out the problems of the past, the present, and the future which might be crippling us. And eventually we tackled the matter of "The Key."

"You are responsible for your own happiness!" My own words echoed in my memory, and I cringed a little recalling how that statement had infuriated *me*!

Kathy had said nothing to me after class. But in the weeks to come we all began to notice subtle changes in her demeanor. She smiled more frequently. She even laughed now and then.

"What's happened to you, Kathy?" I bravely questioned her at last, no longer able to contain my curiosity.

"I guess I've just learned how to be thankful, Lee. The idea that I was responsible for my own happiness really made me stop and count my blessings. And now, every time I get on the emotional skids, I try to remember to thank God out loud for every single good thing that I can possibly think of!

"That verse from Philippians 4 really set me on the right track. In fact I've memorized it now: 'Finally, brethren, whatever things are true, honest, just, pure, lovely, of good report, if there is any virtue, any praise, *think on these things!*' "

Kathy paused, and I stared at her, marveling at her simple faith. "And you know what?" she went on, with a beautiful smile on her face. "In spite of everything—and I mean *everything*—there's a whole lot more good in my life than there is bad!"

The kids sing it in Sunday school. Remember? "I've got the peace that passes understanding down in my heart ... down in my heart to stay." At last Kathy's got it. Lee's got it too.

# AN UNHURRIED LIFE: THE PRACTICE OF "SLOWING"

## JOHN ORTBERG

— from *The Life You've Always Wanted* —

*"People nowadays take time
far more seriously than eternity."*
(THOMAS KELLY)

N OT LONG AFTER MOVING to Chicago, I called a wise friend to ask for some spiritual direction. I described the pace at which things tend to move in my current setting. I told him about the rhythms of our family life and about the present condition of my heart, as best I could discern it. What did I need to do, I asked him, to be spiritually healthy?

Long pause.

*"You must ruthlessly eliminate hurry from your life,"* he said at last. Another long pause.

"Okay, I've written that one down," I told him, a little impatiently. "That's a good one. Now what else is there?" I had many things to do, and this was a long-distance conversation, so I was anxious to cram as many units of spiritual wisdom into the least amount of time possible.

Another long pause.

"There is nothing else," he said.

He is the wisest spiritual mentor I have known. And while he doesn't know every detail about every grain of sin in my life, he knows quite a bit. And from an immense quiver of spiritual sagacity, he drew only one arrow. "There is nothing else," he said. "You must ruthlessly eliminate hurry from your life."

Imagine for a moment that someone gave you this prescription, with the warning that your life depends on it. Consider the possibility that perhaps your life *does* depend on it. Hurry is the great enemy of spiritual life in our day. Hurry can destroy our souls. Hurry can keep us from living well. As Carl Jung wrote, "Hurry is not *of* the devil; hurry *is* the devil."

Again and again, as we pursue spiritual life, we must do battle with hurry. For many of us the great danger is not that we will renounce our faith. It is that we will become so distracted and rushed and preoccupied that we will settle for a mediocre version of it. We will just skim our lives instead of actually living them.

----------

*Then, because so many people were coming and going that they did not even have a chance to eat, he said to them, "Come with me by yourselves to a quiet place and get some rest" (Mark 6:31).*

# THE JOGGING MONK

RICHARD J. FOSTER

from *Prayer: Finding the Heart's True Home*

ALLOW ME TO TELL you the story of Jim Smith, a former student of mine. Genuinely bright Jim went on to do graduate work at a prestigious school on the East Coast. By the second year, however, he was struggling to maintain his spiritual life, and so he decided to take a private retreat.

He arrived at the retreat house and was introduced to the brother who was to be his spiritual director for the week. Instantly, Jim was disappointed, for under the brother's cowl he noticed jogging shoes ... Adidas jogging shoes! Jim was expecting a bearded sage filled with the wisdom of the ages, and instead he got a jogging monk!

The brother gave Jim only one assignment: to meditate on the story of the Annunciation in the first chapter of Luke's Gospel. That was it. Jim went back to his room and opened his Bible, muttering to himself, "Birth narrative, I've read it a thousand times." For the first couple of hours he sliced and diced the passage as any good exegete would do, coming up with several useful insights that could fit into future sermons. The rest of the day was spent in thumb-twiddling silence.

The next day Jim met with the brother to discuss his spiritual life. He asked Jim how things had gone with the assigned passage. Jim shared his insights, hoping they would impress the monk.

They did not.

"What was your aim in reading the passage?" he asked.

"My aim? To arrive at an understanding of the meaning of the text, I suppose."

"Anything else?"

Jim paused. "No. What else is there?"

"Well, there is more than just finding out what it says and what it means. There are also questions, like what did it say to you? Were you struck by anything? And, most important, did you experience God in your reading?" The brother assigned Jim the same text for that entire day, urging him to read it as much with his heart as with his head. All day Jim tried doing what his spiritual director had instructed, but he failed repeatedly. By nightfall he practically had the passage memorized, and still it was lifeless. Jim felt he would go deaf from the silence.

The next day they met again. In despair Jim told the brother that he simply could not do what was being asked of him. It was then that the wisdom behind the jogging shoes became evident: "You're trying too hard, Jim. You're trying to control God. Go back to this passage and this time be open to receive whatever God has for you. Don't manipulate God; just receive. Communion with him isn't something you institute. It's like sleep. You can't make yourself sleep, but you can create the conditions that allow sleep to happen. All I want you to do is create the conditions: open your Bible, read it slowly, listen to it, and reflect on it."

Jim went back to his room and began reading. Nothing. By noon he shouted out to the ceiling, "I give up! You win!" There was no response, just as he expected. He slumped over the desk and began weeping.

A short time later he picked up his Bible and glanced over the text once again. The words were familiar but somehow different. His mind and heart were supple. The opening words of Mary's response became his words: "Let it be to me ... let it be to me." The words rang round and round in his head. Then God spoke. It was as if a window suddenly had been thrown open and God wanted to talk friend to friend. What followed was a dialogue about the story in Luke, about God, about Mary, about Jim.

The Spirit took Jim down deep into Mary's feelings, Mary's doubts, Mary's fears, Mary's incredible faith-filled response. It was, of course, also a journey into Jim's feelings and fears and doubts, as the Spirit in healing love and gentle compassion touched the broken memories of his past.

Though Jim could barely believe it, the angel's word to Mary seemed to be a word for him as well: "You have found favor with God." Mary's perplexed query was also Jim's question: "How can this be?" And yet it was so, and Jim wept in the arms of a God of grace and mercy.

In the Scripture passage the angel had just informed Mary of her future destiny. What about Jim's future? They talked about this—God and Jim—what might be, what could be. Jim took a prayer walk with God, watching the sun play hide and seek behind the large oak trees to the west. By the time the sun had slipped below the horizon, he was able to utter the prayer of Mary as his own: "Let it be to me according to your word." Jim had just lost control of his life, and in the same moment had found it!

# THE
# ENCOURAGE-
# MENT
## of a
# TEACHER

# ONE FLEW OVER THE TEACHER'S DESK

PHIL CALLAWAY

— from *Making Life Rich Without Any Money* —

*A teacher affects eternity;*
*he can never tell where his influence stops.*
(HENRY BROOKS ADAMS [1838–1918])

WELL, IT'S BEEN quite a week. On Wednesday the children brought home their report cards. On Thursday we went to see their teachers and beg for forgiveness. Sometimes at night, as we sit around the dinner table, I ask the kids, "So, what did you learn today?" Almost without exception, they respond: "Nothing."

This week we had tangible proof that they were telling the truth.

They say that the world will never be a better place until children are an improvement on their parents, and I must admit that though my kids' marks leave a little to be desired, they are a dramatic improvement on mine.

I was a problem child during my school days. In fact, if you were to check the records at Prairie Elementary School, you would discover that I still hold the record for Most Whippings in a Week. If you doubt me, you can talk to my teachers. I believe a few of them lived to tell about it. Of course, I am not proud of this. But let me take the next few minutes to tell you all about those years. And of a teacher who literally changed my life.

---

On my very first day of school, Leslie Kolibaba squealed on me for having my eyes open during prayer (yes, they prayed back then), and teachers viewed me with suspicion from that day onward. By grade three, teachers were already wondering if there was any hope for me. I was known as a kid who couldn't keep quiet, who couldn't keep still, and who couldn't keep from asking far too many questions. I'm sure when they looked around the classroom, they experienced the same anxiety every teacher experiences: Are these kids learning anything at all?

The answer is obvious: No. As proof, here are a few things students have written on tests and essays over the years:

- Benjamin Franklin invented electricity by rubbing cats backward and declared "a horse divided against itself cannot stand." Franklin died in 1790 and is still dead.
- Handel, the famous composer, was half German, half Italian, and half English.
- Bach died from 1750 to the present.
- Beethoven was so deaf he wrote loud music. He expired in 1827 and later died for this.
- Queen Victoria was the longest queen. She sat on a thorn for 63 years. Her death was the final event which ended her reign.
- Socrates died from an overdose of wedlock.
- William Shakespeare was famous for writing and performing tragedies, comedies, and hysterectomies.
- Christopher Columbus circumcised the earth with a 100-foot clipper.
- Our new teacher taught us all about fossils. Before she came to class I didn't know what a fossil looked like.

By the time I reached high school, I wished for all the world that I could quit. After all, my marks had been slipping ever since kindergarten and few held any hope that I would amount to anything.

To complicate matters, there were some strange teachers roaming the classrooms. One prided himself on calling everyone by birthday. I was July 26. A friend of mine was May 3. "Hi, May 3," he'd say, walking past us in the hall. Or, "July 26, would you stand and read paragraph three from page 220?"

Several years after high school my friend and his new bride were walking around a mall 1000 miles from home, and they happened to meet this former teacher. They stopped to talk with him. But all he said was "Hi, May 3," then he walked away. Needless to say, this dear man's elevator wasn't stopping at all the right floors, and I can't remember a thing I learned from him. Except I never forget my friend's birthday.

Thankfully we had other teachers too.

In tenth grade, I was standing at the drinking fountain swapping jokes with friends, when my English teacher, Mr. Bienert, came along. Taking me aside, he spoke some simple words that have changed my life. Later I discovered that he'd been in the faculty lounge talking to some of the other teachers, all of whom were wondering if there was any hope for me.

"Listen, Callaway," said Mr. Bienert, "your math marks aren't adding up. Your gift at science has yet to be discovered. Biology? Chemistry? Physics? Well, the experiment is not working."

I'd been told this before.

This was not news to me.

But what he said next was the best news I'd heard in a long time: "I want you in my Communication Arts class. I think God has given you a gift in the area of communication."

The very next day I had no trouble getting out of bed. I even put on matching clothes. And after joining his class, I worked eagerly on my very first assignment: writing a poem for a poetry contest. I can't remember a word I wrote, but I'll never forget Mr. Bienert standing at the front of the classroom, pulling five bucks from his wallet, and calling me forward.

"Congratulations, Callaway. You've got first prize," he said, stuffing the bill into my eager hand. "I want you to read this in chapel tomorrow. It's good stuff." The next day my knees knocked and my hands shook, as I walked to the podium. But I read that poem loudly before the entire school.

All because someone believed in me.

You know, I've been influenced by a whole lot of people over the years. Some have scolded me. Some have hollered at me. Some have spanked me. And most have forgotten my birthday. But I want you to remember this: Those who influenced me the most are not those who pointed out all my faults, but those who knew that God was bigger than my shortcomings. Those who influenced me the most didn't just point a finger, they held out a helping hand.

None of us knows what God will do when we encourage someone, do we? I almost flunked French class in high school. Now they're translating my writings into languages like Polish, Spanish, Chinese, and English (one of which I speak fluently). I was born with a face for radio, but a new video series of mine is being distributed in 63,000 churches around the world.

This is no tribute to me.

It is a tribute to the goodness and greatness of God. And it's a tribute to those, like Mr. Bienert, who believed in God enough to believe in me.

We may forget some birthdays. But let's not forget to encourage someone. Today.

# CREATIVE POWER

RICHARD J. FOSTER

from *The Challenge of the Disciplined Life: Christian Reflections on Money, Sex, and Power*

I REMEMBER SO WELL "my pastor." I was young in both years and faith. I was also shy, and to compensate I would often show off and act boisterous. My pastor, however, bore patiently with me through those years of growing. He never tried to make me conform to the religious culture in the trivial matters of dress or speech. He gave me plenty of opportunity to struggle with theological issues, while at the same time setting forth clearly the fundamental tenets of the faith. I was inspired toward faith without conformity, a legacy for which I will always be grateful.

*In the school, power is to be used to cultivate growth, not inferiority.* Let us not kid ourselves; teachers and students are in a power relationship, but it can be a power to lift, not to destroy, if they understand their purpose. When teachers use their authority to stimulate children to learn, to think, to go on an adventure of discovery, they are engaging in a life-giving ministry. But it is very easy for a teacher to push too hard and to criticize too severely; when this happens, the child feels worthless. Teachers need to prod without demeaning, encourage excellence without depreciating those who fall short.

I vividly remember a teacher who prodded me to excellence without demeaning my shortcomings. He was a philosophy professor, and although I cannot remember all he taught me about Plato and Kierkegaard, I will never forget his love of words. He handled words in a way that was new for me: as a treasure to be cherished rather than propaganda to be maneuvered. He had a special regard for the mystery and power of words. In fact, words seemed to usher him into another world, a world in which I was a foreigner. I was very clumsy with words, so his skill with language frightened me as much as it intrigued me. He never depreciated me for my clumsiness but always urged me to try again. And I did try again, until I became at home in this world of words—a world in which zeal and insight meet in friendship, a world in which truth and beauty kiss each other. He was a teacher who saw past my feelings of inferiority and encouraged me to grow.

# THE NEEDS OF CHILDREN

SHARON M. DRAPER

*— from Teaching From the Heart —*

*A Wide Sea and a Small Boat*

*Dear Lord, Be good to me.*
*The sea is so wide and*
*my boat is so small.*

THIS STATEMENT, USED by the Children's Defense Fund, reminds us how fragile and dependent our students are. Whether we teach toddlers or high school seniors, they are pawns in a world they did not make, partners in a game they had no choice but to play. We must remember that children are just that—children. They're not small adults or incomplete pieces of protoplasm. They're kids. They need to laugh and giggle and make mistakes. They need to pretend. They need to dream.

Whether the children are underprivileged and have never seen the inside of a shopping mall, or overprivileged and are given so much they have very little left to desire, they all have dreams. They need love. They need to be touched. They need to know that someone cares. Sometimes the only someone to show that care, the only one with whom a child dares to share a dream, is the teacher.

How does one create a dreamer? Through creativity and imagination. By allowing a child permission to "color outside the lines." By encouraging questions and fostering thought. By creating an atmosphere where dreams can grow and blossom.

What about the children who have failed, not just in school, but in life, the children whose dreams have been destroyed in the dirt? Perhaps these are the children that illustrate the failure of society. I once visited a school that wasn't really a school—it was a jail. These children, ages ten to fifteen, had committed crimes—crimes so heinous that they could not be returned to their families, but had been placed by a judge in this facility for criminal children.

To enter the building, I had to pass through two sets of security checks. Then I was ushered into the bright, colorful reception area. Student-made posters adorned the walls, as in any school. But I saw no students. I was told they were in their cells. "Cells?" I asked. "Yes, cells," I was told.

I was taken on a tour of the facility by a large and cheerful guard. The library. The cafeteria. The gym. It looked like any other school. But it wasn't a school—it was a residential correctional facility. There were guards here, and locked doors, and no access to the outside.

They showed me the rooms where the children slept. Small, bare, almost antiseptically clean. A small bunk with a single mattress, a sink, a toilet, a shelf. And a door with no doorknob that locked from the outside. It was a jail cell.

The children were to meet with me in the area that was used for cafeteria and assemblies. Three rows of folding chairs sat empty, waiting for the children to be brought in. The guards attempted to prepare me before the children arrived.

"They don't get many chances to hear outside speakers."

"Well, I'm glad I'm able to be here for them."

"When they do get a speaker, they usually last about fifteen minutes, and we have to take them back."

"Oh, I thought I had an hour to speak to them."

"You won't last that long. These are really rough characters. But don't worry, we've put on extra guards. You'll be safe."

The "rough characters" were marched in then. Single file. Heads down. Hands clasped behind their backs. A guard in the front. A guard in the back. Totally silent. They sat down quickly in what seemed to be pre-assigned seats with none of the shoving or the usual jostling that accompanies children when they come into an assembly that is exciting simply because it breaks the normal routine. They were being taught correct behavior and had learned not to deviate from it. They did not smile. They wore white T-shirts, dark sweat pants, and slip-on sandals. No shoes with strings.

Guards flanked them on either side of each row. Several more stood at the rear of the rows. They hovered closely, checking for even minor infractions of the rules. They gave me the sign that I could begin.

I looked at the rows of silent faces in front of me. One little boy had freckles and bright red hair. I smiled at him and he smiled back shyly, but not before quickly darting his eyes to the guard standing near. Another boy, with a head full of curly black hair, looked at me like any seventh grader looks at a new teacher—a mixture of doubt and anticipation. Every single one of them looked like kids in any middle school in the United States—kids with adolescent pimples, kids with braces, kids who leave their book bags on the bus. Not criminals.

The first thing I did was to make the guards move back. I wanted to talk to these young people, and I felt no threat from them. I did not know what crimes they had committed. I didn't want to know. All I knew was that they were kids and they were hungry—hungry for praise and a little positive reinforcement.

I started out by telling them stories—stories about some of the people I had met and some of the humorous events during my travels. The stories made them laugh, or reflect, and removed them from their own lives. They didn't have to think about themselves for a few minutes, and both laughter and tears are wonderful relaxers.

One story was about a young man I met at an airport. He carried a map of the airport, an old duffel bag, and one long-stemmed red rose. He asked several people questions, and looked nervous and anticipatory. I watched him for a moment. Then, when he boarded the shuttle train to head to the baggage claim area, I spoke.

"Got a special girl waiting?"

"Yes, ma'am. Is this the train to get a cab? I'm in a hurry."

"Yes, this shuttle will take you to that gate. I'll show you when we get off."

"Thank you, ma'am." He glanced at the rose again, smoothed the wrinkled paper around it, and checked his watch once more.

I couldn't help myself. The boy was about the age of my son. "She must be a very special young lady," I ventured.

The young man smiled then. "Oh no, ma'am. This rose isn't for a girl. It's for my grandma. I ain't seen her in three years."

"Is she sick?" I asked.

"No, ma'am. She's just fine, but I just can't wait to see her. It's been so long."

"Have you been away at college?"

"No, ma'am. I've been in jail."

He was such a fresh-faced kid, so young, so innocent-looking. He could easily have been in my class last year. "Are you glad to be home?"

"Oh, yes, ma'am! I ain't never going back there no more. My grandma raised me, and she tried to tell me stuff about going to school and staying out of trouble, but I wouldn't listen. So I just want to go see her and thank her and tell her I love her. She's all I got in the world."

The shuttle stopped then, and he bounded off to head for a taxi. "Give your grandma a hug for me!" I called to him. He turned, grinned, and promised he would.

Many of the children I was speaking to on that day had been raised by grandparents. I could see the look of fond recollections on their faces. Then I told them about Zak.

I was tired and frustrated. I had spent several hours in the Charlotte airport because of a cancelled flight. When the plane was finally ready to board, I asked if I could get my seat changed from an aisle to a window. All I wanted was a quiet spot. I dragged myself on the plane, hoping, in spite of the screaming babies all around, that I could just lean my head against the window and sleep for a few minutes.

When I got to 12A, a little boy was sitting there, next to his grandmother. His arms and legs, obviously badly burned, showed many scars of multiple grafts and layers of mottled skin.

"Hi, I'm Zak."

"Hi, Zak," I replied gently.

"Is this your seat, ma'am? Zak wanted to ask if he could have the seat by the window," his grandmother said to me.

"Sure, Zak, take the window. I love sitting in the middle seat."

"I'm five years old today! You know, I was four yesterday, and today I'm five! I don't see how that happened! I was four for such a long time. I was getting tired of being four, and now I'm five. It's about time!"

"Well, Happy Birthday, Zak. Enjoy sitting by the window. Where are you from?"

"I'm from Conway, South Carolina, and I just got back from Cincinnati."

"Cincinnati?" I asked the grandmother.

"He goes to the Shriners Hospital there. That's where he gets the treatments for his burns. He got burned when he was eight months old—grabbed a cord of an electric frying pan and pulled hot grease all over him. Sixty-eight percent of his body was burned. Praise the Lord his face got spared, and his groin area—(them Pampers don't burn!), but the rest of his little body was almost destroyed."

She told me about the private jet that the Shriners sent to pick Zak up when he was burned, how he was burned at 8:00 P.M. and by 1:00 A.M.

he was in Cincinnati in treatment. She told me how he was not expected to live, but they tried some new treatments and he rallied. They fly back and forth from South Carolina to Cincinnati on a regular basis for his grafts and treatments, and all of it is paid for by the Shriners Hospital. I have lived in Cincinnati all my life, and never knew what a wonderful job they do with kids like Zak, who was charming, energetic, and learning to fight unbelievable obstacles in his young life.

I forgot how tired I was, and was ashamed of myself for complaining about such mundane inconveniences as a late plane flight. I told Zak I was a teacher, and he was fascinated because he was going to start school in the fall. We talked about school for a bit, and I told him what he could look forward to, like reading, and making friends. He was quiet for a moment, and then he said to me, "You get to talk to a lot of kids in your job?"

"Yes, I get to talk to young people all over the United States—even South Carolina."

"Well, when you get a chance, would you tell them something for me?"

"Sure, Zak. What would you like for me to say?"

"Tell them to be really careful around fire."

"I will, Zak. I promise."

They understood about kids with problems. They understood about obstacles. They sat rapt and fascinated, while I told tales and gave them subtle encouragement. Forty-five minutes had passed. The guards made no move to end the session. Finally, I asked the young people for questions.

They wanted to know about my school, my students, my children at home, my age. (Kids always ask that one.) Then finally, the red-haired, freckle-faced boy in the front row raised his hand. He asked me the hardest question I have ever been asked, even by the best Washington and New York reporters.

"If you could give some advice to us in here," he began, "what would you tell us?"

The room was silent. Never had I faced such a difficult question. I thought for a minute, then took a deep breath.

"Tell them to stay in school," I heard a voice whisper behind me. It was the director of the facility. The kids heard it, and I saw their shoulders visibly slump.

"I'm not going to tell you what your director wants me to say," I said slowly, ignoring the director's snort of disapproval behind me. The kids sat up straighter, listening. "I'm going to tell you something that will last a little longer." Even the guards were rapt with attention.

"You cannot change your past. What has happened to you, and what you have done can never be changed. It is the past and it is gone." They were with me, their faces reflecting their thoughts.

"Your present is not very pleasant, but it is a place where change can take place. It is a place where decisions can be made and wounds can be healed. It is a place of transition." They were starting to move uncomfortably in their chairs.

"Your future is a glorious rainbow if you want it to be. You have the power to make your future anything you want it to be. You have the strength within yourselves to create your future. Never let anyone or anything remove that from you. You have the power to fly!"

I could tell by the looks on their faces that they believed me. Many of them had tears in their eyes. Most of them shook my hand when it was over. Some gave me hugs. They needed the warmth of another human being. The guards marched them back out to their cells then, again single file, hands behind their backs. But as they left, they held their heads up high, and they smiled at me as they marched out of the door.

# A Change of Heart

## NANETTE THORSEN-SNIPES

I LOVED MY FIFTH-GRADE teacher until I wrote a poem. I worked a week on the poem and once my teacher read it, she raved about it to the class and to other teachers. That same day I rode the bus home, practically walking on water.

Both of my parents were thrilled that I, a quiet, unassuming student, had received such accolades from my teacher.

The next morning upon returning to the classroom, my teacher asked me to step outside the door. "Where'd you get the poem?" she asked. The tone in her voice frightened me, but I answered as truthfully as I knew how.

"I wrote it." I could feel my heart thumping in my chest.

"No you didn't," she said, tapping a ruler against her hand. "Mrs. Grant said she saw that same poem in a book."

"She couldn't have," I insisted, "I wrote that poem."

My teacher's eyes narrowed and she sternly said, "Don't lie to me, young lady."

I didn't flinch, and I never backed down because I had not lied, but the teacher took my hand and marched me to the principal's office, where I sat for the rest of the day. And where I endured deep humiliation.

For the next few years, I refused to write anything creative. In the tenth grade, I landed in Mr. Cleary's class, a man I greatly admired. I liked him so much that I did everything I could to show off my creative ability. So when he announced we had to make book reports, I threw everything into mine so it would stand out—and it did.

"Nanette," he said curtly one morning, "I want to talk to you." I'd heard that tone of voice before and steeled myself against the coming barrage.

"You copied your book report, didn't you?" he asked.

"No sir, I didn't." My palms began sweating, and I rubbed them together.

"Yes, you did, but if you'll redo it, I'll let it go this time."

I started to argue with him, but I knew it wouldn't matter what I said because teachers were always right. I had learned that long ago.

My heart ached when I said, "Yes, sir." I took the paper and, sitting at my desk, I dumbed down my own writing until it was acceptable.

Later that year, Mr. Cleary announced we would have a creative writing contest—a "fiction" contest. I wanted to shout, "Yeesss!"

Finally the day came, and we spent an hour of class time writing our stories. This was the year that the urban legend of "The Hook" was rampant and scaring teenagers throughout the schools. I decided to write about "The Hook," and turned my classmates into main characters. I built up the scenes, but instead of horror, I changed it to humor. When the hook touched the car door, it changed miraculously to a coat hanger wielded by one of my classmates. With trepidation, I handed it in.

The next day, Mr. Cleary said only two of the stories were worth sharing. He called one of the boys to read his story. My classmates clapped.

Afterward, Mr. Cleary sauntered toward the middle of the class with the other paper. He walked directly to me and placed it in my hand. I remember looking at him quizzically.

"Read it," he said.

I stood. My knees shook beneath my skirt. At first, my voice quavered too. Then I propelled myself into the story. When I was through, the kids jumped to their feet and applauded.

"Good job," he said. I could feel the love of God radiating from Mr. Cleary's heart when he later apologized for not believing I could write.

At the end of that year, I brought my yearbook for Mr. Cleary to sign.

A tear glistened at the corner of his eye as he wrote, "I wish I could have had a special English section for you, Nanette. The next two years should see you develop into a really fine writer. Thanks for helping make this year such a fine one for me."

Many years have passed since that day. But Mr. Cleary had kindled a passion in my soul, and when God's own creative work—the Bible—stoked my heart later, my love of the Lord blazed in the stories I've told. And published.

SECTION ELEVEN

# THE
# *INFLUENCE*
# *of a*
# TEACHER

# PAUL TOURNIER: THE POWER OF THE PERSONAL

J.  KEITH  MILLER [1]

⟶ from *More Than Words* compiled by Philip Yancey ⟶

A "C-MINUS!" I couldn't believe it! I'd been a good student all my life and had spent hours developing, writing, and editing this, my first sermon for a homiletics class in seminary. I was angry, but, more than that, I was confused. This sermon represented the way I had always thought preachers should preach, sharing their own personal experience, strength, and hope along with the biblical message. But my professor of preaching had dismissed my sermon as being unacceptable.

After pointing out some structural mistakes that I could agree with, he leaned back in his chair, drummed his fingertips together, and said, "The reason your grade was a C-minus was because you were 'personal.' You used the first person singular to describe the problems with which you were dealing." He paused and then went on. "In the first place, using the first

---

[1] Keith Miller is a widely known lecturer and author. His more than fifteen books include the best-sellers *The Taste of New Wine*, *The Becomers*, *Please Love Me*, the recently published *The Secret Life of the Soul*, and several books cowritten with his wife, Andrea Wells Miller, and Bruce Larson.

person singular in a sermon is *not effective*. And besides, it is not in good taste." He pushed my sermon across the smooth surface of the large desk.

Still, in the years to come I could not shake the notion that one's own feelings and experiences of pain, fear, anger, guilt, shame, sadness, and joy could be drawbridges over which a communicator could carry the message and love of God into the deepest levels of people's lives. I felt that the world and the church had become depersonalized and that people were growing more and more isolated. Somehow the stance of the "expert" communicator expounding abstract concepts or telling laymen how they should live seemed to further the depersonalizing process. Worse, the message of God's healing love didn't appear to be catching the attention of the modern world—even many of those already in the churches.

I knew that what I needed personally was a model: someone who was seriously trying to be God's person and to have intellectual integrity but who also faced the kinds of fears, problems, and failures that I faced. Evidently, this was not a combination to be found in a single Christian communicator. People seriously committed to God either did not have the kind of struggles I had or considered them too insignificant to be mentioned. I had met some other strugglers who, like me, were trying to slug it out with this paradox, but we were all nobodies. I had never run across a communicator with any authority who admitted to this strange predicament of feeling unable to be whole, in spite of the power and joy to be found in the gospel.

Then, in 1965, Dr. Paul Tournier came to Laity Lodge in the remote hill country of southwest Texas for a conference. I was director of the conference center. And although I had heard of Paul Tournier, I had never read anything he had written.

The first evening he spoke, the "great hall" at the lodge was filled with psychiatrists, psychologists, M.D.s of all varieties, Christian ministers, and lay leaders from various professions. The air was almost electric with expectation, and I realized how much the conference guests were looking forward to hearing this man whose books they had read. Many of the guests had traveled hundreds of miles for this weekend. We had turned down a number of requests to attend, and still the group had overflowed into the motel in the nearest town. As we all gathered for the first session, I wondered how well Tournier would be able to cross the language barrier from his French through an interpreter to us. I had no idea what content to expect.

Then he began to speak. Within five minutes the room had faded, and we were transported into another world. A little boy was describing his struggle with loneliness and self doubt almost sixty years before in a country several thousand miles away. You could have heard a pin drop on the stone floor. I sat behind the speaker near the huge fireplace and looked past Paul Tournier into the eyes of almost a hundred sophisticated American professionals. Inside those eyes, wide open, I could see a roomful of other lonely little boys and girls reliving their own struggles for identity and worth.

After fifteen or twenty minutes had passed, a strange thing began to happen, something I have never seen happen before or since. As Paul spoke in French, we found ourselves nodding in agreement and understanding— before his words were translated. We trusted him so much, and felt he understood us so well, that we knew at a subconscious level we would resonate with what he was saying. He described problems, doubts, joys, meanings, fears—many of which still existed for him—and spoke of them naturally, as if they were the materials God normally worked with in his healing ministry among all people, Christians included.

Before us was a man who did not even speak our language, a man in his sixties who wore a wrinkled tweed suit, and was exhausted from a whirlwind trip across America. And yet as he spoke fatigue, age, clothes, and language difference all faded into the background. He turned periodically to make eye contact with those of us behind him. I was mainly conscious of his sparkling eyes, his personal transparency, and a glow of genuine caring about his face. As he spoke, I felt and heard love, and the truth of God about my own life.

I found myself having to fight back tears—tears of relief and gratitude, and release from my solitary burden. Because of my own struggles, I had sensed that, to be healed, we need more than good medical advice or even excellent psychological counseling. We need presence. Vulnerable, personal *presence*. I knew the Bible claimed that was what God gave us in Jesus Christ and the Holy Spirit: his own presence to heal and strengthen us. And I had felt that somehow we Christians were to be channels to convey that healing presence personally to other people's lives through our own openness and vulnerability. But in Paul Tournier I met at last a living model of the kind of communication I was trying in a stumbling, uncertain way to find.

I made two decisions during that conference. First, I would go back to school to get some psychological training. Second, as soon as I finished a manuscript I was working on, I would read some of Tournier's books. I was already in the process of writing a book for new Christians about living in a personal relationship with God. Other books of this sort seemed to me overly pious, and they did not deal with the "stumbling blocks" that had bothered me as a new Christian. After Tournier's visit, I completed the manuscript of that, my first book, with great enthusiasm.

And when I sent my manuscript to the publisher, the next thing I did was to read *The Meaning of Persons*. Again, tears. For years I had been looking for books whose authors were real and transparent so that I could identify with their problems and move toward healing in Christ. The closest thing I had found was Augustine's *Confessions*, which is what had finally persuaded me to write a book about my own struggles as a contemporary Christian. But if I had read Tournier first, I doubt I would have felt the need to write that manuscript, *The Taste of New Wine*.

Knowing that a man existed who loved God and yet who also faced his own humanity and used the discoveries and methods of scientific investigation did something for me. And knowing that, at least partially because of Christ, this man could afford to be honest about his own struggles helped push me far beyond my small horizons of security and faith.

From that day forward Paul Tournier became a mentor and friend, until his death in 1986. We traveled and spoke in conferences with other Americans and Europeans in Spain, Portugal, Italy, and Greece. His work has influenced me deeply. But more, his life and his way of personal dialogue gave me a direction for living as a Christian which has brought more hope and courage than I could have imagined.

# DECEPTION, INTEGRITY AND BLACKMAIL

BOB STROMBERG

from *Why Geese Fly Farther than Eagles*

IN 1962, WHEN I WAS a ten-year-old towhead, I attended Mrs. Saiers' fifth-grade class in my little town of Canoe Place. I liked Mrs. Saiers a whole lot, and I thought she liked me, too.

On the second day of school, Lorna Culver and I were chosen to work on the bulletin board out in the hallway. It was a privilege to do so, and only Lorna and I, two out of thirty-one students, were chosen. It's true that when I had volunteered, I sat as still as possible, staring ahead with a stone expression, my arm straight up and motionless. But that's not why Mrs. Saiers chose me. I knew it was because she liked me.

Lorna and I were given free rein over the art closet. Toward the end of each year, the art closet—and art class for that matter—became a little discouraging. Miss Owen, our part-time, roving art instructor, was an innovative teacher. But it had to be difficult at the end of the year to come up with two months of creative ideas of things you could make with empty glue bottles and tacks. But today, the eighth of September, the closet was full of colored construction paper, crayons and even a bottle of glitter (the first I'd ever seen).

Lorna and I decided to make a large "Welcome Back" sign, surrounded by falling leaves, footballs and, in keeping with the autumn theme, a small triceratops in the upper corner (the dinosaur was my idea).

Lorna was up on the ladder, fastening the last falling leaf, when I discovered a tack that had no point. It was just the head, which, lying flat in my palm, created an illusion of severe pain.

"Oh, Lorna," I feigned, "look at my hand. Oh, no! I can't stand it!"

It's remarkable what gravity can do to an unconscious body. Lorna hit the floor like a lump of warm clay, just as Mrs. Saiers came through the door.

"Well, children, how are my artists?" she said with a smile, not yet noticing that one of us was dead. "Oh, my goodness! Lorna! Dear!"

Mrs. Saiers knelt down and rolled Lorna's limp body over. "Bobby, what happened?"

"I-I d-d-don't know," I trembled, tears filling my eyes. "I just showed Lorna my . . ." And opening my hand for Mrs. Saiers to see, I watched at about three-quarter speed as her face turned the color of a dirty chalkboard, and she rolled her eyeballs back in her head, sharing a part of herself with me I'd never known. Lorna was just coming to when Mrs. Saiers sort of slumped down on top of her. This was a brand new experience for Lorna, too, who now lay in the corner beneath her sleeping teacher.

If this had happened the year before in the fourth grade, my teacher, Mrs. Fudd, would have reprimanded me sternly and carried me by the skin on the back of my neck to the principal's office. My principal, Mr. Peligrini, would have looked over my shoulder as I copied a letter to my parents expressing my sincere desire to transfer to a nearby military academy.

But for some reason, Mrs. Saiers liked me. "Oh, you character!" she said with a faint laugh as Sherry Sullivan, who wanted to be a nurse when she grew up, daubed Mrs. Saiers' forehead with a wet paper towel.

What more proof did I need that she liked me?

A few days later, at an all-boys' assembly program, Mr. Peligrini told us fifth-graders he was looking for "a few good young men." He encouraged us to be all that we could be and find our future as patrol boys.

He said, "Ask not what your school can do for you; ask what you can do for your school."

I didn't know why he said that line with a funny accent. But it didn't matter; I was stirred by his speech and felt I had something to strive for. The patrol boys were an elite group of the very best Arnold Avenue School had to offer. Only twelve boys were chosen from the fifth and sixth grades to be highly trained in pedestrian safety. They carried long, menacing poles with red flags tied to the end, and they wore pure silver, state-issued badges on white patrol sashes across their chests and were given the authority to stop irresponsible students at the crosswalk and report vagrants directly to Mr. Peligrini. They were Mr. P's handpicked squad, and nobody messed with the patrol boys.

It was rumored, though I never believed it, that on being commissioned, each boy was told Mr. Peligrini's first name. I didn't believe any child knew Mr. P's first name. During the twelve years he had been the principal, perhaps as many as 150 boys had gone through the patrol ranks. If that many knew his first name, surely some deviant junior higher would have leaked it by now. But no one had.

At least twice a month, we were given blue mimeographed sheets to take home to our parents. As a distribution ritual, all of us would take the sheets passed over the head of the student in front of us, shove the whole pile to our noses for a whiff, remove the top one for ourselves, and "two-hand" it overhead to the student behind. (We had been doing this for years, and we did it well.) Then we would scan the copy informing our parents of an important meeting of the PTA. At the bottom we would read the signature, L. Peligrini, Principal.

Often when the hall was filled with children and Mr. P was at his post, one of the older boys would look slightly past him and shout down the hall, "Hey, Larry" or "Hey, Leonard." The boy hoped that Mr. Peligrini would look his way and therefore reveal the truth. But he never did.

The patrol-boy selection process would take two weeks. Mr. Peligrini would watch us all carefully, and consulting with our teachers about our academic progress and in-class behavior, he would make his selections. These would be posted on the bulletin board outside the main office.

I had never wanted anything so badly in my life. To think I might be given the privilege of getting up in the dark on winter mornings and walking to school through blizzards that would turn back lesser boys. That I would enter the school early with Mr. Lewis, the custodian, and, together with the "chosen few," select my pole from the closet marked "Mr. P's Patrol." That I would walk proudly eight or nine more blocks to "my corner," where I would serve my principal, my school and my country.

And that wasn't all! After two years of flawless service, I would board a yellow school bus before dawn and ride seven hours to Washington, D.C., where, together with my squad, I would be given a four-hour tour of the White House; the Capitol (both the House and the Senate); the postal department; the Treasury; Arlington Cemetery; the Washington, Jefferson and Lincoln Memorials and eat a free bag lunch before returning home.

My hope was exhilarating, but my fear weakened my knees as I stood with at least fifty others, watching Mr. Peligrini post the tiny list. It read:

1. Capt. Mark Rackish—Arnold Ave. east corner
2. Craig Mundy—Arnold Ave. west corner
3. Barry Burgason—Maple St.
4. Mark Elliot—Broad St.
5. David Kanally—Chestnut
6. Dale Caskey—Keating Ave.
7. Bobby Stromberg—alternate

A small group cheered. Most just walked away. I stood there in disbelief, my eyes full of tears, sobs threatening to burst through my chest. I felt a hand on my shoulder.

"So, Bobby, are you proud you made the squad?"

It was Mrs. Saiers, who obviously didn't understand. Being an alternate wasn't exactly "making the squad." The alternate was only called on if a regular was sick. Everyone knew that due to greater responsibilities and the resultant heightened resistance to viral strains, patrol boys were hardly ever sick.

Only once in my memory had an alternate been promoted to full-time service, and that was when one of the regulars moved away. But the family names on this list had lived in Canoe Place almost since the beginning, and I knew they weren't going anywhere.

But that wasn't what bothered me most. At that moment I didn't care that I wouldn't be able to sacrifice my early morning sleep and after-school playtime, or even that I would miss out on the best trip of my life. It was that the other boys had been deemed worthier than I.

"I just don't get it," I said with a sob. "I just don't understand. Mr. Peligrini said he would watch us closely. What did he see in me that wasn't good enough?"

"Oh, Bobby," she said, kneeling down and wiping my eyes with her doily, "I'm sure it's not that you're not good enough."

"Well then, what is it? Why did he pick these—"

And then the truth hit me so hard I nearly lost my breath. Anger burned through my brush cut, igniting little fire needles on my scalp. Right before my eyes, I saw in the list what Mr. Peligrini had hidden so well with his rousing speech to all of us boys.

He knew all along who would be chosen. I had been deceived. It had nothing to do with our behavior or our work. The squad had been chosen by their street addresses. Right down the list it went.

"Rackish and Mundy, Arnold Ave.," I mumbled. "Kanally, Chestnut. Elliot, Broad. Caskey, Burgason . . ."

They all lived near the corners they had been assigned.

As I looked from beneath my brow, I saw the same truth hit Mrs. Saiers. Her jaw dropped, and she became that chalky color I'd seen only weeks before.

"Excuse me," she said, forcing a smile as she tried to conceal her shock.

"You need to run along, and of course, I have some things I need to do." Then almost cheerily, "Congratulations; see you in the morning."

She walked into the office and, without knocking, marched directly through the door marked "L. Peligrini."

As the glass rattled in the slammed door, I heard the muffled, arguing voices of my teacher and principal.

Mrs. Saiers: "mufflemufflemufflemuffleShocked! You told those boys thatmufflemufflemuffle."

Mr. P: "Now, now, I muttermuttermuttermuttermutterGeographic considerationsmuttermutter."

This went on for quite a while as I stood by the bulletin board. I wasn't where I could see into the outer office, but I could hear enough to know I shouldn't be there. Finally the door flew open, and Mr. Peligrini's black, polished shoes, echoing on the hardwood floors, came quickly. There was no time to shoot for the front entrance or even run the six steps to my classroom.

"No, Mrs. Saiers!" he snapped, stopping for emphasis. And then coming again, "We will not discuss this further."

Then he was there, his solid gold belt buckle right in my face. The buckle had a fancy swirl forming the letters "LP."

It all happened so quickly. I looked up prayerfully into Mr. P's astonished face. Mrs. Saiers rounded the corner, completely unaware of my presence.

Loudly she protested, "But Leslie!"

Mr. Peligrini closed his eyes and sighed with his whole body, the way a criminal might do. He realized he had been caught, and there was no reason to continue the game. It was all over.

Mr. Peligrini's first name was Leslie! There was no doubt in my mind that I was the only child in the history of Arnold Avenue School to know the truth. Not even the patrol boys, under sworn oath and the threat of dishonorable flunking, could have kept this secret. The man's name was Leslie!

I did not understand the concept of blackmail, but I think Mr. Peligrini and Mrs. Saiers did.

Trying hard to conceal her amusement, my favorite teacher said, "Mr. Peligrini, I think it would be so much safer if we had one more patrol boy posted by the bus entrance. Don't you agree?"

Still motionless, staring toward the ceiling, he answered, "Yes, Mrs. Saiers, I think Bobby could begin tomorrow morning."

I became a patrol boy because Mrs. Saiers was willing to become my advocate. Until this event, I'd never realized that adults could be unfair and dishonest, even toward children. I might have become angry and then bitter or distrusting, and, who knows, that might have changed my whole life. But Mrs. Saiers would not allow it to happen.

I liked Mrs. Saiers a whole lot, and I knew she liked me, too.


P.S. Patrol boy wasn't all it was cracked up to be. Neither was our trip to Washington. What I remember most is throwing up on the bus.


P.P.S. I never told his name.


P.P.P.S. Until now!

# By Way
## of Hope

GENE BECKSTEIN

As told to Gloria Cassity Stargel

*In 1950, as a twenty-nine-year-old new Christian,*
*I had lots to learn. God sent me the perfect teacher—*
*young Billy Graham.*

THE POSSIBILITY NEVER entered my mind that someday I
would be a teacher. In fact, the possibility was slim that someday I
would amount to *anything* worthwhile.

Born in the tenements of Buffalo, New York, I grew up with no hope
of better days. Violence there was a way of life. When I was eight, the
thunder of gunshots woke me. Looking out the window, I saw a man die
in the glare of a streetlight. Oddly, it didn't seem that unusual.

We knew little of law and order. Even in our apartment, brawls often
erupted. Our dad was a part-time prizefighter and a full-time alcoholic.
Combined with seven brothers, that made for a real physical family. Following the tradition, at thirteen I beat up a guy and spent eighteen months
in a training school.

After serving my sentence, I rejoined my street buddies stealing hub-
caps—and anything else we could find. Later, many of them either died in

jail or from alcohol and drug abuse, products of an impoverished neighborhood that knew only hopelessness and despair.

Somehow I scraped by in high school. Then, after trying a few no-future jobs, I joined the Marine Corps. Four years of military service opened a new door for me. For the first time, I learned that there *was* a life beyond the ghetto. But that life required education. The G.I. Bill paid tuition for veterans and I accepted—my one-way ticket out of the slums by way of New York University.

I was a twenty-nine-year-old college freshman when a friend tricked me into going to Rochester to hear some guys sing. He didn't tell me the program would be in a church—a place foreign to me. After the singing ended, a giant Purdue football player spoke. John Ducharte was six feet five, 255 pounds, and talked about being intimate with Jesus Christ.

Having played a little minor league baseball, I wanted to meet this dude—another athlete. After the program I walked up and shook John's hand. "Do you really believe all that rubbish?" I blurted out.

"I certainly do," John said, then added, "Do you have a minute?"

I followed him into a little room, where he pulled out a couple vinyl chairs. We sat down and he opened up his Bible. "Of course you know John 3:16, don't you?"

I lied. I said yes. John Ducharte saw right through me and started reading that verse from the Gospel of John. "For God so loved the world, that He gave his only begotten Son, that whosoever believeth in him should not perish, but have everlasting life (KJV)."

Then he read Romans 10:13. "For whosoever shall call upon the name of the Lord shall be saved."

About then the door burst open and John's little four-year-old daughter swooped in. He didn't scold her for interrupting. Instead, he put his big arm around her and gave her a kiss.

I was embarrassed. I had been taught that real men don't do stuff like that, especially in front of another man!

Before I could recover, John's wife rushed in. "I'm sorry, John," she began. But he just put his other arm around her and kissed *her*. I marveled at that scene, those two muscular arms around his loved ones. This man had something special, something I'd never seen before.

After the ladies left, John asked if we could pray, this time putting that huge arm around *my* shoulders. When this guy prayed, I glimpsed *God!* For the first time I saw that it was possible for ordinary people, even street people like me, to get to know God on a personal basis.

I cried.

"What's the matter, friend?" asked that gentle giant.

"I feel terribly far away from God," I managed.

He replied, "Good."

"What's good about that?"

"Because," he explained, "that's what Jesus is all about. He's the bridge to God. He's the mediator. You want God to come into your life—Jesus is the bridge. Would you like that?"

"I know I want whatever it is that you've got," I told him. Right on the spot I prayed to accept Jesus Christ into my life. And that life has never been the same.

Back home in Buffalo, I found an old, inner-city church where the people accepted me. Barely a month later, another door opened when I returned to Rochester, this time as athletic director at a youth camp.

Leading the Christian training there all week were young, just-starting-out Billy Graham, Cliff Barrows, and George Beverly Shea. What a privilege for a brand-new believer, getting to work with those three. We were all put to the test, though, as rain played havoc with our schedule. I grumbled because I couldn't lead the outside activities I had planned; the youth were boisterous with no way to work off excess energy. Yet the Graham team remained calm and patient. I learned much from their worship sessions. I learned even more from their actions.

I could hardly wait to tell others the good news of Jesus. My opportunity came soon thereafter when I landed a part-time job at a Buffalo radio station. Each day I did ten minutes of news, often bad news. Then—

with a quartet standing by ready to sing Gospel songs or someone to give a Christian testimony—I'd say, "But hang on, we've got some 'Good News at Noon!'"

After college, I migrated southward and devoted the next thirty-seven years as a public school teacher, administrator, and counselor. I coached high school baseball, basketball, and soccer. Often, while working with students—students in trouble with the law or the school—I called upon the patience Billy Graham taught me years earlier. And I called upon the memories of my ghetto days—the anger, the frustration. Most of those young people needed to know God's love just as I did.

I retired in Gainesville, Georgia, and returned to the ghetto. This time, however, I went to help *others* find a way out. My wife, Margie, and I sold our home across town and moved into a little house next door to the Melrose Housing Project so that we could be accessible to the people.

When I decided to start a feeding program at Melrose, Margie made the meatloaf, a neighbor furnished green beans and corn bread, and we put out the word: "Anybody hungry is invited to lunch." So it was that "Good News at Noon" was reborn.

I began working with all age groups, facing their many needs: countless hungry and homeless, gang-related trouble, drug and alcohol addiction, AIDS, frightened children who endure family strife.... I saw again that insidious problem that prevails among those born into poverty, a problem I knew only too well—*hopelessness.*

I particularly wanted to reach the children, to somehow build in them self-esteem. I *know* how that child feels who gets on the school bus with not so much as a pencil, only to have to compete all day with children who sport shiny new lunch boxes. Remembering how John Ducharte helped change my life by telling me of God's love, I wanted to do the same for the children and their families.

Gradually, surprisingly, volunteers began to appear. Today, fifteen years later, they number in the hundreds—professionals and lay people, civic clubs and churches. We receive no federal money. Instead, business groups organize fund-raising golf tournaments; school children collect canned goods; groups coming to serve meals bring the food with them; physicians retire, then contribute their time, skills, even equipment. All desire to share the Good News: The Gospel of Jesus Christ.

Good News at Noon now feeds hundreds every day, provides a homeless shelter, medical clinic, and dental clinic. Volunteers teach, mentor, and counsel. Each person who receives physical or mental help receives spiritual help as well. We tell each one, "God loves you. God's love can give you hope—hope, and help, for a better life."

God is blessing. Many lives have been turned around—drug addicts rehabilitated, jobs regained, families restored, little children playing without fear.

These are proud people; they just need a little help. I try to serve them in a non-judgmental manner, because someone once saw some worth in me. Thank you, John Ducharte. And thank you Billy Graham, Cliff Barrows, and George Beverly Shea. Thank you for sharing with me—the Good News.

# $\mathscr{M}$AN OF
# FEW WORDS

## ELAINE ERNST SCHNEIDER

B ECAUSE I WAS AN extremely verbal child, growing up with my dad was an experiment in linguistics. My father was a man of few words. Whenever I wanted my dad's permission for an activity, I planned a speech that included who would be there, where it would take place, how long it would last, and why it was an incredibly wonderful opportunity for me. He would listen and then say either "yes" or "no." There were never any qualifiers, no "yes, but be home by dinner" or "no, unless you can convince me otherwise." It was simply yes or no.

I remember being particularly frustrated with my father's "no" answers. I always presented my best argument, supporting my position with facts and logic. But my father didn't debate with me. He'd say, "Didn't I already tell you no?" If I persisted, Daddy would sigh. "No, Elaine, end of report." And that was that.

My father's phone messages were also lessons in patience and long-suffering to a teenage girl. In high school, I actively participated in National Honor Society projects, club meetings, choir practice, and play rehearsal. I was also a class officer. Not only did I enjoy being involved in all of these areas, but I also came into contact with many gorgeous teenage hunks. One bountiful day I met two great guys and gave each of them my phone number.

The first words out of my mouth when I walked through the front door were "Dad! Did anyone call?"

His answer, of course, was the one word, "Yes."

I was not about to accept that as complete information, so I queried for a more accurate description of the caller.

His answer? "A boy."

Since I had met *two* guys that day, this did not help me. I ran to my room in tears.

And such was life with my father. Taciturn, straight to the point, no unnecessary information—that was Daddy.

Knowing my dad's aversion to words in general and his predisposition to terseness, it surprised me to hear that my father was going to teach the eleven-year-old boys' Sunday school class. Not only did my dad take the class for the initial segment of time for which he was asked, but he taught that class for many years. I always wondered if he actually said anything, or if they all just sat in their chairs and stared at each other. I was sure that if someone were waiting on my father to break the ice with sparkling conversation or a springboard comment, then he'd be sorely disappointed. Still, September after September, my father hung his sign outside the Sunday school room: Mr. Ernst—Eleven-Year-Old Boys.

I never understood why the boys kept coming to Daddy's class. And I could not fathom what they saw in my father that made them want to *talk* to him. I reasoned that these guys simply did not know my father as I did. They could not appreciate what living with my dad was like, having never been the recipients of one-word answers or unidentifiable phone messages from potential dates.

Indeed, when I was a junior in high school, I met another one of those hunks. Larry was a big ol' boy, as my daddy called him, the halfback for his high school football team. We dated all of my junior year and were still going together when Larry was drafted by Darrell Royal to play football for the University of Texas in Austin.

By this time, I was a high school senior. University of Texas was having a great football season and Larry invited me to come for a big end-of-the-season celebration. I arranged for Dad to drive me to Austin and to attend the game with me. Then I would be Larry's date for the after-game activities.

Dad and I made the drive and arrived on campus just as the football team was entering the athletes' dining hall. As a mere high school student, I cringed at the thought of entering a college dining hall and having the entire University of Texas football team staring at me, no doubt thinking, "What is that high school girl doing in here?"

But my dad was undaunted. He marched right in and I followed sheepishly.

Larry was busy eating and didn't even notice us. I stood frozen, my thoughts paralyzed by my insecurity. Then from across the room, I heard a shout and watched as the quarterback for the University of Texas ran across the room and threw his arms around my father. "Mr. Ernst," he yelled, "Is that you?"

"Hi, Allen," Dad answered. "Have you found a church down here yet?" The man of few words had spoken.

By then, the football players were gathering around my father as Allen introduced them to the Sunday school teacher he had as an eleven-year-old boy. For the first time, I saw my father as the godly man that he was. He had taught Allen to love God, and that mutual love for the Savior linked them to each other.

Years later, I worked full time on a church staff as a children's minister. The hardest task before me each summer was to recruit the children's Sunday school teachers for the following autumn. I honestly had to beg for teachers. No one wanted to teach the young ones. After all, they were just children. What could it matter?

It matters. Eleven-year-old boys grow up to be young men. My father may not have been the most verbal man on the planet, but he knew how to communicate a sense of decency, fine character, and goodwill. Daddy's faith was grounded on God's Word, and he lived a life that was a role model to young boys like Allen. Perhaps the sign outside my dad's Sunday school room *should* have been changed. It might have better reflected what went on within the class if it had read: Mr. Ernst—Man of Few Words—The Right Ones.

# THE
# COMPASSION
## of a
# TEACHER

# A GIFT OF GRACE

TERRI WILSON WEAVER

I HAD SPENT A PLEASANT afternoon reminiscing with my favorite teacher. We'd talked about the time he'd run into my father, an electrician, at a local diner. He had told my dad that I was struggling with understanding electricity and I was too proud to ask for help. We'd laughed that after fifteen years I still had the old physics book he had given me so I could underline and write notes in the margins because I retained things better that way.

Removed from the constraints of public school and the roles of teacher and student, our talk had turned to our faith in God and the impact it had on his teaching. How he tried to live his faith even though he wasn't allowed to speak it in the classroom.

As my little girl played on the floor, we sipped iced tea and sat side by side on his couch looking at his photo album. Mr. Roberts was that kind of teacher, someone who cared enough about his students to keep photo albums of us. Coming across a picture of me with my best friend he commented, "I remember you girls getting really mad at me that year. I know you didn't speak to me for a while. But I can't for the life of me remember why."

I sat for a moment in stunned silence. I couldn't believe that he'd forgotten, I remembered it so clearly. It was probably the most important lesson I learned from him that year.

During my senior year of high school I was a leader in my class, president of two clubs, and a teacher's aide. I had a good rapport with all my teachers, and I was headed for college on an academic scholarship. I was making good grades, had a great job *and* my own car. Life was good. The only problem was, I was a cheat. I had it rationalized in my head and I'd have denied it.

My best friend and I had worked out a system in junior high. I was great in science while she excelled in math, so we decided to complement each other's weaknesses. She did the math homework, I did the science, and we would swap. We studied together for every test so that both of us maintained a high average and the teachers never figured out our scheme. They never would have figured it out if I hadn't messed up.

Every six weeks we turned in our notebooks in physics class. It counted for a third of our grade. That particular six weeks in physics had included intensive math, so my friend had done double duty. I'd been coasting along carrying a B average and not worrying about much. When I turned in my notebook that morning I neglected to remove the photocopy of her homework.

Mr. Roberts was my mentor and the advisor for the science club. He'd been my teacher for two years. I'd known him since I was a little girl. He was more than my teacher and my mentor—he was my friend. I can only begin to imagine his disappointment when he opened my notebook that day.

The day he returned our notebooks he didn't say anything about anyone having been caught cheating. He didn't shame or humiliate me. He simply placed my notebook on my desk as always. I felt as if I had been punched in the stomach when I opened the cover to find the missing photocopy emblazoned with the words "See me" in red ink.

It took me the entire day to muster the courage to face him. When I walked into his empty classroom late that afternoon I didn't know what to say. So I went with the obvious. "You wanted to see me?"

He looked at me for a long moment, disappointment darkening his eyes and said only one word, "Why?"

In that instant, I saw the truth. I had let him down, I'd let myself down, and I was going to fail the six weeks and probably lose my scholarship to college. But I at least owed him the truth. Barely above a whisper I responded, "Because we thought we could."

He replied flatly, "You can go."

I was utterly mortified. There I was, president of the science club, president of the math club, and for years I'd been cheating my way through both subjects. I'd rationalized it with the excuses that "everyone does it" and "if I wasn't learning the material I'd never have been able to pass the tests." But the hard truth was I'd been cheating and now I was caught. I'd been caught by my teacher, my mentor, my friend. I left the building, went to my car, and cried.

Mr. Roberts and I hadn't said ten words to one another in days. The following Monday, Mr. McCoy, another science club advisor, finally confronted me, "What is going on with you and Harvey?"

Haltingly, I told him the whole story and I said, "I'm going to resign as science club president."

"Oh, no you are not! You're going to go over there across the hall and you're going to talk to Mr. Roberts and you are going to make this right!"

I desperately wanted things to be right again and I knew better than to argue with him, so I swallowed hard and went across the hall.

Mr. Roberts was sitting at his desk on the far side of the room. I stood in the doorway for a long moment and then stammered, "Mr. Roberts, I need to talk to you . . ."

He looked up as I started across the room toward him, tears already streaming down my face.

Like the father welcoming home the prodigal, he got up and met me halfway. He held out his arms, and I buried my face in his shoulder and began to cry in earnest.

"I'm so sorry! I'm so sorry, Mr. Roberts! I'm so sorry!" He let me cry it all out babbling all the while, "I didn't mean to ... I'd talked myself into believing that we weren't really cheating ... I know I let you down ... I'm so sorry!"

When I finally stopped sobbing he handed me his handkerchief and said quietly, "I know, Terri Beth. It's okay."

A huge weight lifted off my chest. I was still going to fail physics, but our relationship had been restored.

Since the day Mr. Roberts handed my notebook back I'd begun to rework that homework set, more for myself than anyone else. I had to know that I could do it on my own without cheating. Later that afternoon I brought the redone homework to his room. He took it without comment, but he smiled. From that day on it was as if the incident had never happened. It was forgiven and forgotten.

Two weeks later we got our report cards. I hated to look at it, knowing I was going to have an F in physics and knowing that I deserved it. But I finally opened the report anyway. There, beside the word Physics, in bold black ink, was a B—a grade we both knew I had not earned.

Now, fifteen years later as we sat in his living room, I realized again how blessed I was. How like Christ, the gentle teacher, Mr. Roberts had been. When he confronted me with what I had done to offend him, there was no shame placed on me. When I came to him, when the first words of apology were said, he came to meet me with open arms. When what I deserved was punishment, he chose to forgive and beyond forgiving, to bless me. So completely had he forgiven me that he didn't even recall what I had done. Even as I reminded him of the cause of our conflict, he put his arm around my shoulders and told me he was proud of me. There was no condemnation. Twice I had been given a very special gift. Each time it had been a gift of grace.

# HARRY'S EYES

PATRICK BORDERS

I CAN'T CONTROL THESE children. What makes me think I can teach them?"

The problem started for Ivy Collins on her first day at the Detroit School for Crippled Children. She arrived early to her second-floor classroom. Looking out the window, she watched the buses pull in with disabled children from all over the city. Two men, the driver, and an assistant stepped off the first bus and carried a young boy in a wheelchair. They wheeled him to the building and carried him up the stairs to the classroom. Many of the children who followed had little or no use of their legs and had to be brought in the same way.

One by one, the students filed into Ivy's room. Passing in front of her were children suffering from paralysis, arthritis, congenital deformities, and other disabilities. Many of them also struggled with some form of mental retardation. There were thirty children in all.

She nervously patted her hair as she smiled at her students. *How will I ever manage?*

"Okay, class," Ivy said, "let's quiet down and sit still while I check attendance."

The children ignored her. Sarah, a blond six-year-old, moaned for no apparent reason. As Ivy walked toward her, two eight-year-olds, Robert and Charlie, raced their wheelchairs to the top of the stairs.

While she tried to corral the two boys, Harry yelled, "I hate school! I hate school!" He thrashed his long arms against the sides of his wheelchair. Ivy would later learn that Harry was prone to seizures that made his arms shake uncontrollably. Because he had problems sitting still, couldn't hold a book or turn a page, he had never learned to read.

At home that night, Ivy stayed up late wondering how she'd ever teach these children. She eventually fell asleep and dreamed of Harry screaming, while Charlie and Robert crashed down the stairs in their wheelchairs.

Every day brought more chaos. In class, she raced from desk to desk, trying to control her students' behavior and teach them something; at home, she succumbed to nightmares. She had studied countless teaching methods in college, but none of them worked. Her years of training and a degree in education had failed to make a difference.

After the last day of the semester, she packed her things and headed home for Christmas break thinking, *I can't do this anymore.* Christmas morning came, and as she opened her gifts, she thought of the small, helpless child who came to save us all. "Whatever you did for one of the least of these . . . you did for me" (Matt 25:40). She summoned her courage and decided to finish the school year.

During lunch on her first day back, a commotion erupted from the far side of the room. "I hate mashed potatoes!" Harry yelled. She walked over to him and saw his face splattered with food. Ivy realized the problem. It wasn't that Harry hated potatoes, but he'd lost control of his arms and couldn't feed himself. He flailed his head from side to side as he screamed.

Ivy took his napkin and gently wiped his face as he continued jerking his head. Sitting down opposite him, she asked, "May I help you eat, Harry?"

He didn't answer.

She scooped a spoonful of potatoes and held it in front of his face.

Slowly, Harry stopped thrashing, and he opened his mouth and took the bite.

As she fed him, Ivy gazed into his watery green eyes. He blinked rapidly. Harry was obviously trying his best to keep from crying. Ivy felt her own tears welling up. In her mind, the angry, spastic boy faded away, and in his place sat a boy who was struggling just as she was. Their problems were different; their struggles were similar. This boy was special—a child of God. The more she studied his eyes, the more she saw the frustration showing through.

In that instant, Ivy discovered a secret—an almost magical method that would transform her students and her teaching. She carefully observed the faces of all her children as she taught class that afternoon. When she worked with them individually, she bent down in front of their desks and peered into their eyes—searching for the special child inside. The more she did this over the next few days, the more she understood their unique personalities. Every face presented a window into a new world of thoughts and emotions.

She visited Harry at his home and observed the interaction between Harry and his mother. When talking with Harry, his mother always made eye contact and smiled as she spoke in a slow and loving voice. Harry laughed and played during the visit and showed no signs of his usual anger. Ivy also visited her other students in their homes, and each time, she learned more about them.

She attended every continuing education class on disabled children she could find. At lectures presented by local hospitals, she learned more about the medical conditions of her students, and especially, what it was like for a child to experience these ailments.

During that second semester, Ivy focused not on Harry's behavior, but on the special child she had come to know. Harry's shaking episodes grew less frequent. One day, he wheeled himself to the front of the room. He sat straight and calm as he held a children's book and read to the class.

Ivy beamed. *This is where I belong.*

She continued to deal with things that wouldn't occur in a regular classroom. Over time, she learned what teaching methods worked for each child, and her students learned to respond to her care and direction.

Ivy had the heart of a teacher; she knew she couldn't reach her students without getting to know them. For over thirty years, she loved her job, and she loved her kids. She gazed into their eyes and sought out the wonderful children living inside.

Ivy Collins was my grandmother, and she often told me about her early days as a teacher. When I remember her stories, I'm reminded of the way God seeks out the unique child in all of us. Too often, we don't feel special. We're like Harry, thrashing about, exasperated with our handicaps. Then we sense God peering into our eyes—reaching into our soul. That's when we feel his love, and we know that we're special.

# My
# TOMBSTONE

PHIL CALLAWAY

— from *I Used to Have Answers, Now I Have Kids* —

IF I HAD TO PICK my favorite year in school, I'd take grade five in a minute. In fact, I spent four very fine years there. (Just kidding.)

This was the year Miss Weismuller came to town to conduct experiments in our classroom. I was one of those experiments. In September, she assigned me a spot behind Bobby Spaulding (a brilliant and discerning young man who laughed at all of my jokes) and across the aisle from a weepy girl with horn-rimmed spectacles and a name I can't recall. I was moved around the classroom after that, like a wandering Gypsy, without home or country, and by January I had developed a fond dislike for the strap. I suppose I did not care for Miss Weismuller, either. She was too strict—I felt—and her lips were puckered, as if she spent her evenings sucking buttons off a sofa. I pointed these things out to my mother one evening and received a clear message: "She's your teacher, Philip. You may not like her, but you will show her respect. She has been put there for a purpose and ... um ... I'm sure we will one day know what that purpose is." I wasn't quite sure what Mom meant, but I knew her sentiments were not shared by all the parents.

In mid-March, one mother stormed angrily past the principal of our Christian school, past Miss Weismuller and into our classroom. There she removed her son—books, pencils, eraser, and all. He never returned. Moved clean out of the district, some said. We students watched with interest as the dust settled and, strangely, found ourselves siding with Miss Weismuller. For the next fifteen minutes we listened to her every word, refrained from joke-telling, and kept quiet without being told. But such things come to an end, and for me the ending was high in drama.

"Put your books away, *ja*," said Miss Weismuller, as the clock wound down to 3 P.M. "It is time for our Bible memory test." The words struck horror into my ten-year-old heart. Once a month we wrote out verses from the Bible, and our marks were clearly reflected in our report cards. My marks had been slipping ever since kindergarten, and this month they were destined to slip even further. I had been too busy with lesser things to store away Scripture. And so, I slid some verse cards from my desk, lodged them on the chair between my legs, smiled saintlike at the weepy girl across the aisle, and in desperation, began to cheat on my Bible verses.

Believe it or not, this is what I wrote: "My little children, these things write I unto you that ye sin not."

I stopped, looked at the blackboard, and hoped I hadn't been writing too fast.

The verse continued: "And if any man sin we have an advocate with the Father, Jesus Christ the righteous: And he is the propitiation for our sins: and not for ours only, but also for the sins of the whole world."

The other children were writing dutifully. A few were scratching their heads and furrowing their brows. I continued: "And hereby we do know that we know him, if we keep his commandments. He that saith, I know him, and keepeth not his commandments, is a liar, and the truth is not in him. But whoso keepeth his word, in him verily is the love of God perfected." I even wrote out the reference correctly: I John 2:1–5 KJV.

Sleep was slow in coming that night. Oh, my report card would be looking better, but in the darkness tidy report cards don't hold a candle to clean consciences. *You are a liar, Phil, and the truth is not in you.* Quietly I made my way into my parents' bedroom and tapped my mother on the shoulder.

She sat up straight. "Palestine!" she said, then breathed deeply and asked, "What's wrong?"

"Nothin'," I replied.

"Son, it's almost midnight . . . what's the matter?"

"Mom," I said in muffled tones, "I cheeddonahuhm."

"You what?"

"Ah Mom, I cheated on my memory verses."

She got out of bed and knelt beside me. We talked and then we prayed, asking God's forgiveness. I was leaving the room feeling a whole lot lighter—when Mom stopped me in my tracks: "You will have to tell Miss Weismuller, too."

About an hour later I drifted fitfully in and out of a dream that haunts me to this day:

The punishment is administered in the schoolyard, in the heat of afternoon recess. The children are lined up alphabetically, according to height. Ministers from the surrounding area gather, wearing black suits and solemn expressions. The mayor is there. He introduces Miss Ida Weismuller's speech, and all the schoolchildren listen attentively. "We are gathered here today to witness the conclusion of an awful blight on each one of our reputations, *javol!*" The younger children strain their necks to get a good look at me. The older ones simply nod their agreement and look away. Bobby Spaulding isn't laughing. Miss Weismuller isn't finished: "Today I have learned that Philip Ronald Callaway cheated on his Bible memory verses." A collective gasp arises. The girl from across the aisle removes her horn-rimmed spectacles and dabs the corners of her eyes. Miss Weismuller continues with little emotion: "Let each of us resolve to conduct ourselves in an obedient and orderly fashion, with sobriety and prudence, lest we end up like this poor young man. This . . . this . . . *cheater.*"

The children file past me in a solemn procession, from the youngest to the oldest. Each is handed a stick, which they toss with a sigh into a pile around the swingset leg to which I am tied. The ministers strike matches and toss them on the sticks. Emotionless, Miss Weismuller fans the flames. With my report card.

No, I did not sleep well that night.

The small graveside service held the following Tuesday is attended by my parents only. My sister and brothers are too ashamed to come. They study algebra instead. He cheated on his Bible memory, they remind each other in hushed tones. But in later years they sneak into the graveyard late at night, their flashlights searching out my tiny tombstone and the words:

THE UNKNOWN STUDENT
1961–1971

*For habits he would not break*
*He was ceremoniously burned at the stake*
*His sins are too many to list*
*He certainly will not be missed.*

*May we rest in peace.*

The next morning I crept bleary-eyed into the school building. Early. The other students weren't there yet, but Miss Weismuller was. She waited inside the courtroom, gavel in hand. I tapped on the door. "Come in," said a thick accent. I opened the door obediently. She sat behind her desk, dressed mostly in black. My judge. My jury. My executioner.

"What is it?"

I forced myself forward and stood still before her. "I came to tell you that ... I'm sorry," I said, unable to look up. "I ... um ... cheated on Bible memory yesterday."

"And how did you cheat, Philip?"

"I copied off the verse cards."

"Did anyone see you?"

"I don't think so."

"Did God see you?"

I looked up for the first time. "Yes," I said. "He kept me awake last night."

Tiny traces of a smile formed around her eyes. "Then you've asked His forgiveness, *ja?*"

"Yes."

She smiled widely in spite of the bun in her hair. "Then I forgive you, too," she said. "After school today you will take the test over, but I forgive you."

From that day on, I didn't cheat on another test. Oh, I was accused of it once in high school. I got 73 on a math test, and my teacher said, "No way." But I didn't do it. And I think I know why. You see, way back in fifth grade a teacher who had every reason to pronounce judgment smiled. And offered me grace.

> *You are a liar, and the truth is not in you.*
> Yes. But God forgave me.
> *You cheated on Bible memory.*
> Yes. But I told Miss Weismuller. And she forgave me, too.

Thanks to that forgiveness I won't have the previous epitaph etched on my headstone. I've had a lot of years to think about it, and this is what I'd like my tombstone to say:

> *He found God's grace*
> *too amazing*
> *to keep to himself.*

It seems Miss Weismuller taught me more than either of us expected.

If I had to pick my favorite year in school, I'd pick grade five in a minute.

# TWO SOMETHINGS DEEPER

### BOB BENSON

from *See You at the House*

I HAVE A FRIEND whom I know casually. I had met him a time or two before and I saw him again toward the end of the summer. He was wearing a neck brace and was kind of hunched up. He didn't look like he was having much fun that day.

I took counseling in seminary, so I know how to get stuff out of people. Using one of my best counseling techniques, I said, "Did your wife hit you?" No response.

So I went to a deeper, more probing statement. "You thought they said 'Stand up' when they really said 'Shut up', didn't you?" That didn't elicit any response either, so finally I said, "Aw, come on, tell me what happened."

"Well," he said, "I'm kind of embarrassed to but I will. My son and I were up the street at the neighbors where they have a new swimming pool. They had invited us to swim and we were diving off the board. I really hate to tell you this but I hit my head on the bottom. Really, it knocked me out. If my son hadn't been there to bring me to the surface and drag me up on the wall, I probably would have drowned."

You've probably noticed that I have a quick mind—like a steel trap. Right away, I knew what had happened to him. Although I didn't share this precious truth with him, I knew the scientific principle involved. He ran out of water before he ran out of dive. He looked like it, too.

In our Sunday school class one morning, we were talking about the depth of the love of God. How deep is his love? How deep will it really go? Someone said, "It goes as deep as you go."

I said, "Well, that's okay, except I want to add another phrase, if you don't mind."

Since I had the microphone and I was the teacher, they said I could add another phrase. "I want to say it goes as deep as you go and two somethings deeper. I don't care what. Two inches, two feet, two miles, two somethings. It is always down there just below you."

For whatever it is that plagues you, maybe some dark deed that would startle and shock us all, maybe a steady accumulation of the same thing, I want to write this very plainly. There are always two somethings deeper still. Forgiveness is not forgiveness unless it is unconditional.

One night I came in very late and the family was all in bed. In the playroom by the door on the table in a puddle of light from an overhead lamp was a note. It was like a little poster because there was some artwork on it. It said, "Dear Dad, I did something bad today. I am sorry. Please forgive me."

Tom, the writer of that note, has a little of the con man in him, too, because it also said: "PS. I love you. Tom."

So I went upstairs to make the rounds, and to kiss my family and whisper to their sleeping forms that I love them, and I went into Tom's room. Tom doesn't ever wake up or even answer. He just sits up in the bed so quickly after you kiss him that you have to duck to keep from getting hit. It took a moment to get him back on his pillow and to put the covers up under his chin. He still didn't even know I was there. Kneeling by his bed, I whispered softly into his unhearing ear, "Tom, you are forgiven."

Some might ask how I could forgive when I didn't even know what he had done yet. It is really simple. He can't do anything for which I won't forgive him. He has "blanket" coverage.

You don't have to carry the weight of your past into your tomorrows. And you can't run out of water before you run out of dive. Forgiveness is always two somethings deeper.

# PERMISSIONS AND ACKNOWLEDGMENTS

Every effort was made to secure proper permission and acknowledgment for each story in this work. If an error has been made, please accept my apologies and contact Bethany House Publishers at 11400 Hampshire Ave. S., Minneapolis, MN 55438, so that corrections can be made in future editions.

Permission to reprint any of the stories from this work must be obtained from the original source. Acknowledgments are listed by story title in the order they appear in the book. Heartfelt thanks to all the authors and publishers who allowed their work to be included in this collection.

## THE NURTURE OF A TEACHER

"The Alchemy of Dream Day," excerpted from *Dream* by Mark Rutland, pages 9–13. Copyright © 2003 by Mark Rutland. Used by permission of Charisma House, a part of Strang Communications Company, published in 2003. All rights reserved.

"The Simple Fruits of the Spirit," excerpted from *See You at the House* by Bob Benson. Copyright © 1986 by Peggy Benson; all rights reserved. 3404 Richards Street, Nashville, TN 37215. Used by permission. All rights reserved.

"I Never Knew Her First Name," by Cecil Murphey. Copyright © 2003. Used by permission. All rights reserved. Cecil "Cec" Murphey has written or co-written more than 90 books including *Gifted Hands* and *The Relentless God*. Disney Studies has purchased the film rights to *I Choose to Stay*, which was condensed in *Reader's Digest* magazine.

"Buddy Films," by Rusty Fischer. Copyright © 2003. Used by permission. All rights reserved. Rusty Fischer is a freelance writer who lives and works in sunny Orlando, Florida, with his beautiful wife, Martha. His work has appeared in *Chicken Soup for the Soul, Stories from the Heart, God Allows U-Turns,* and most recently *The Heart of a Father.*

"That Extra Mile," by Anita Higman. Copyright © 2003. Used by permission. All rights reserved. Anita Higman is an award-winning author who writes for children and adults. Her sixteenth and seventeenth books came out in 2004. One of her co-authored books won its second award, and Anita has won two volunteer awards for her contribution to literacy. She lives near Houston with her husband, Peter, and two children. You can find out more about Anita Higman and her books at *www.anitahigman.com.*

## THE EXAMPLE OF A TEACHER

"Patience," excerpted from *Simple Words of Wisdom* by Penelope J. Stokes. Copyright © 1998 by Penelope Stokes. Used by permission of J. Countryman, a division of Thomas Nelson, Inc.

"Brief Encounter," by Suzanne Schryver. Copyright © 2003. Used by permission. All rights reserved. Suzanne Schryver was a high school administrator, teacher of English, and running coach for ten years before becoming a stay-at-home mom to her three children. She is a freelance writer of both fiction and nonfiction. She resides in New Hampshire with her family.

"Silver Threads Among the Gold," by Lanita Bradley Boyd. Copyright © 2003. Used by permission. All rights reserved. Lanita Bradley Boyd, Fort Thomas, Kentucky, draws from her years of teaching, church ministry, and family experiences. She has stories in the *God Allows U-Turns* series, *Rest Stops for Teachers, The Heart of a Mother,* and articles in a variety of publications, including *Teaching K–8, Christian Woman,* and *Parent Life.*

"Miss Ritter's Bible," by Lucia St. John. Copyright © 2003. Used by permission. All rights reserved. Lucia St. John is a novelist, poet, and artist residing in New Jersey. Her writing has appeared in numerous publications throughout the world, including *Moody Magazine, Show and Tell,* and *Broken Streets.* She and her husband are the parents of two children.

## THE DISCIPLINE OF A TEACHER

"Back of the Room," by Nancy Ellen Hird. Copyright © 2003. Used by permission. All rights reserved. Nancy Ellen Hird's articles and short stories have appeared in numerous magazines for children and adults. She is also the author of "Marty's Monster" and "Jessica Jacobs Did What?" Nancy says that she has experienced "back of the room" times. They have been seasons of learning and growth.

"The Ugly Truth," by Kay Dew Shostak. Copyright © 2003. Used by permission. All rights reserved. Kay Dew Shostak is the president of the American Christian Writers Group in Atlanta. She and her husband, Mike, have three teenagers, which may explain why Kay enjoys writing fiction to escape. She is currently seeking publication of her first novel.

"Chosen," by Jeff Adams. Copyright © 2003. Used by permission. All rights reserved. Jeff Adams is a freelance writer and inspirational speaker. Jeff's stories have reached millions of readers. He has been published online in connection with *The Wall Street Journal.* Jeff lives in Arizona with his wife, Rosemary, and their daughter, Meaghan.

"Tough Love," by Cia Chester McKoy. Copyright © 2002. Used by permission. All rights reserved. Cia Chester McKoy hopes this compilation wins out over apple knickknacks as a teacher's gift. A freelance writer and speaker living near Milwaukee, Wisconsin, Cia has a kind, tolerant husband, five noisy older teens, and an unfinished memoir keeping her busy. Feel free to contact her at *ciamckoy@earthlink.net.* A version of her story was published by Broadman & Holman in *Rest Stops for Teachers,* ed. Susan Titus Osborn, 2003.

## THE STRENGTH OF A TEACHER

## THE LESSONS OF A TEACHER

## THE PROVISION OF A TEACHER

"An Act of Legislature," by Joy Clary Brown. Copyright © 2003. Used by permission. All rights reserved. Joy Clary Brown, married to Wayne Brown, is a minister's wife and mother to Meri Beth and Molly. Joy is a speaker, author, former teacher of the deaf, and entrepreneur. Through *Words of Joy*, Joy develops Bible studies that challenge and inspire. She is also a speaker with Women by Design.

"Experimental Lessons," by Twila Sias. Copyright © 2003. Used by permission. All rights reserved. Twila Sias teaches in the education program at Florida Christian College in Kissimmee, Florida, where she desires to help students develop not only knowledge and skills but also a teacher's heart. Though not a professional musician, she continues to enjoy playing the piano.

## THE LOVE OF A TEACHER

"People Change People," by Keith J. Leenhouts. For information about the very effective volunteer court mentor movement of some eight million volunteers, 1959–2003, write Retired Judge Keith J. Leenhouts, 830 Normandy, Royal Oak, MI 48073 *www.courtmentor.org*. Information about the book, *Father, Son, 3-Mile Run* and the latest book on court volunteer mentors, *Misdemeanors and the Miracle of Mentoring*, is also available from Leenhouts. Story originally appeared in *Father, Son, and a Three-Mile Run* [currently out of print].

"Persistent Love," by Candy Arrington. Copyright © 2003. Used by permission. All rights reserved. Candy Arrington's publishing credits include *Focus on the Family, Marriage Partnership, The Christian Communicator,* and *Writer's Digest*. She is coauthor with Dr. David Cox of *Aftershock: Help, Hope, and Healing in the Wake of Suicide* (Broadman & Holman 2003). Candy and family live in Spartanburg, South Carolina. *www.CandyArrington.com*.

"I Love You More Than Crayons," by Pepper J. Stinson. Copyright ©
2003. Used by permission. All rights reserved. Pepper Stinson has
taught public school for twenty-five years and is currently a primary
teacher at Augusta Independent Schools. She's also been a pastor's wife
and mother of two boys. She keeps busy in her church's music department and she teaches an adult Sunday school class. Recently, she and
her husband have become in-laws and empty-nesters. Her passions
include chocolate and playing the piano.

"Love It Back to Life, Mother," taken from *First We Have Coffee* by Margaret
Jensen. Copyright © 1995 by Harvest House Publishers, Eugene, OR
97402. Used by permission.

## THE INSPIRATION OF A TEACHER

"Revenge of the High-School Math Teacher," excerpted from *The Words That
Inspired the Dreams* by Caron Loveless. Copyright © 2000 by Caron
Loveless. Used by permission of Howard Publishing Co., West Mon-
roe, LA. All rights reserved.

"The Stranger Who Taught Magic," excerpted from *A Touch of Wonder* by
Arthur Gordon. Copyright © 1974 by Fleming H. Revell Company.
Used by permission of Fleming H. Revell Company, a division of
Baker Publishing Group. All rights reserved. The poem, "On the
Dunes," by Sara Teasdale, was originally found in *Collected Poems of Sara
Teasdale*, published by The MacMillan Company, New York, New York.
The book appears to be out of print and the rights have reverted to
the estate of Sara Teasdale.

"Grace Notes," by Jeanne Zornes. Copyright © 2002. Used by permission.
All rights reserved. Jeanne Zornes, of Wenatchee, Wash., passed on her
love of music to a guitarist son and violinist daughter. She's a CLASS-
certified conference speaker and award-winning author of hundreds of
articles and seven books, including one on encouragement titled *When
I Felt Like Ragweed, God Saw a Rose* (Kregel).

## THE WISDOM OF A TEACHER

## THE ENCOURAGEMENT OF A TEACHER

## THE INFLUENCE OF A TEACHER

as children's pastor and teacher. Her work has been seen in *Whispers from Heaven, Cup of Comfort,* and *Catholic Digest.* Presently, Elaine writes children's curriculum and is managing editor for Lesson Tutor, an online resource for teachers and parents. She is the author of *52 Children's Moments.*

## THE COMPASSION OF A TEACHER